HOT TUBS, SAUNAS, & STEAM BATHS

Hot Tubs, Saunas, & Steam Baths

A Guide to Planning and Designing
YOUR HOME HEALTH SPA

ALAN E. SANDERFOOT

Storey Publishing

The mission of Storey Publishing is to serve our customers
by publishing practical information that encourages personal independence
in harmony with the environment.

Edited by Deborah Balmuth and Andrea Dodge
Art direction by Cindy McFarland
Cover design by Kent Lew
Text design and production by Jessica Armstrong
Front cover photographs by *(left to right)* ©Dan Gair/Blind Dog Photo, Finnleo, MrSteam
Back cover photograph courtesy of Hot Springs Spas
Interior photo credits on page 147
Illustrations by Terry Dovaston
Indexed by Andrea Chesman

Printed in the United States by CJK
10 9 8 7 6 5 4 3 2 1

Library of Congress Cataloging-in-Publication Data

Sanderfoot, Alan E.
  Hot tubs, saunas, and steam baths / by Alan E. Sanderfoot.
    p. cm.
  Includes index.
  ISBN-13: 978-1-58017-549-4 (pbk. : alk. paper)
  ISBN-10: 1-58017-549-X (pbk. : alk. paper)
  1. Hot tubs. 2. Sauna. 3. Vapor baths. I. Title.

TH6501.S265 2005
690'.896—dc22

2005013282

C O N T E N T S

A Warm Beginning

ew things are more comforting than a warm embrace, whether it comes from a loving parent or an old friend. And when we can't get that calming touch from another person, we often seek out cozy refuge beneath a down comforter, next to a roaring fire, or submerged in a hot bath.

In stressful times (of which there seems plenty), it's natural to want to cocoon, to wrap oneself in a warm and protective environment. New-age psychologists might say it's our natural desire to return to the womb, the most protective environment we have ever known. Well, they may be right, especially given the rate at which people are flocking to health spas to be massaged, wrapped, steamed, and soaked in an attempt to feel rejuvenated — I dare say *reborn* — in mind, body, and spirit.

Today, incredible numbers of people are lured to health spas. In 2004 alone, Americans visited spas an estimated 136 million times for some form of coddling, according to the International SPA Association. So it's no real surprise that an increasing number of homeowners are trying to recreate the spa experience under their own roof with spas, saunas, and steam baths. In fact, the number of visits to destination spas has stagnated in the past few years, partially because more people are creating spa environments in their own homes.

Let's take a brief look at where it all began. Today's home spa industry has roots in ancient Indian, Greek, and Roman culture. According to Sanskrit sources, Hindus practiced Ayurveda more than five thousand years ago. *Ayu* means "life" and *veda* means "knowledge." Hence, *ayurveda* can be defined as the knowledge of life. Using the curative properties of plants and essential oils, Ayurveda aims to relieve naturally the stress, tension, and negative emotions of daily life. Among the prescribed tasks, depending on one's disposition, is a sweat bath. Many Ayurveda treatments are incorporated in today's spa therapies. Indeed, it's no coincidence that when Austria-born Horst M. Rechelbacher, who holds an honorary doctorate in Ayurveda from Gurukul Mahavidyalaya Twalapur, Haridwar University, founded his company in 1978, he called it Aveda, now the most recognized brand in the health spa industry.

Better known than the Hindus for their bathing rituals are the Greeks and Romans. In fact, Homer mentions the Greeks' passion for bathing in the *Iliad*. Greek and Roman rulers considered it one of their basic responsibilities to provide social and recreational activities for the populace. Hence, gymnasiums and adjacent baths became as ubiquitous in ancient Rome as shopping malls are today. The first of these baths served individual neighborhoods and were called *balnea*. Their immense popularity prompted rulers to create opulent *thermae*, massive communal baths that could accommodate

The Turkish Bath (1862) by Jean Auguste Dominique Ingres is an extraordinarily sensuous depiction of communal bathing in the 19th century. Completed when the artist was 82 years old, the widely reproduced masterpiece resides in the Louvre in Paris.

thousands of bathers at the same time and included facilities for exercise and sports, food vendors, and attendants who offered the modern-day equivalent of spa treatments. Not to be outdone, each emperor strived to create even grander *thermae* than his predecessor, using marble, colorful mosaics, and precious metals to adorn these impressive spaces and their magnificent vaulted ceilings. And to ensure the ruler's popularity, entrance fees were minimal so nearly everyone could afford admission.

In ancient Rome, the baths were a way of life. Every afternoon throngs of people — men and women, young and old, aristocrat and pauper — concluded their workday with a trip to the baths. Bathing became a symbol of Rome, something that made them feel superior to other societies. That attitude might have been supercilious, but one has to give the Romans accolades for their architectural and engineering prowess. The baths were essentially a series of rooms and pools, all warmed by *hypocaust*, a system that heated the raised floors and walls by channeling heat and steam from wood fires through a network of earthenware pipes. The system was so effective that the baths' water and floors could be heated beyond the boiling point. To prevent heat blisters on their feet, bathers often wore sandals.

The Roman bath was ritualized, and bathers proceeded through a series of rooms in a specific order. First was the *apodyterium*, the dressing room where bathers would leave their clothing under the watchful eye of a servant or slave. Next was the *palaestra*, or gymnasium, where bathers were oiled down before performing exercises. From here, patrons moved into the *frigidarium* for a cold plunge bath. Then it was quickly on to the *tepidarium*, or warm room. The *caldarium*, or hot room, was next. This steamy chamber contained a hot plunge bath (or *labrum*). After some time in the soothing mist, the bather would have a servant or friend scrape off the oil from the bather's skin using a special tool called a *strigil*.

Homer and other writers tell us that the Greeks also enjoyed the hot-air bath, called *laconicum*. Though many people attribute the sauna concept to the Finnish, it was the people of Laconica, the ancient region of Greece whose capital was Sparta, who conceived the idea of creating a hot-air bath by heating rocks. Today, however, the sauna is synonymous with the Finnish lifestyle, with more saunas per capita in Finland than cars.

After the *caldarium* or *laconicum*, the Roman bather would return to the *apodyterium* via the *tepidarium* and *frigidarium*. The bather might then take a brisk swim in the *natatio,* or outdoor swimming pool. To keep the baths as clean as possible, aqueducts, an engineering marvel borrowed from the Greeks, brought fresh, clean water to the city and other areas of the empire.

Like many modern health spas, the ancient baths catered to a culture that thrived on pleasure and leisure. However, they were also used for medicinal purposes. Often a physician would prescribe a particular room at the bath for a patient to visit, depending on his or her diagnosis.

Despite their reputation for healing the sick, the baths were not endorsed by Christians, who called the *thermae* "cathedrals of flesh." During the Dark Ages, the stately sanctuaries fell to ruin. Unfortunately, it took centuries for western Europe to rediscover the healthful benefits of hot-water baths, dry-heat baths, and steam baths. And recent years have brought the most dramatic advances in hot tub, sauna, and steam bath technology. What were primarily amenities for four-star hotels, fitness clubs, and health spas are increasingly making their way into homes across America.

Whether you're interested in hot tubs, saunas, steam baths, or all three, this book

▲ At the ancient Roman baths, patrons moved from room to room to experience cold-water plunges, hot-air baths, steam baths, and a variety of other spa treatments.

strives to demystify these products and bring you up to date on everything you need to know to create the ultimate home spa environment, from purchasing and installation to maintenance and repair. For more than a decade, I've been writing about trends in these areas, and I know firsthand what you're getting yourself into, including the things that make you say "ooh," "ah," "uh-oh," "wow," and "huh?" These products are not inexpensive, so a little education can save you a lot of money and headaches.

As I write this introduction, my 102-degree hot tub beckons me with its soothing waters and instant hydrotherapy. And inside my master bathroom, a tile and glass-block steam shower stands ready to envelop me in its hot, misty fog. It's only a matter of time before I make room for a sauna. Yet, as excited as I am about my own home spa, I'm more excited for you, the reader, because you are planning (or at least considering) bringing a hot tub, sauna, or steam bath into your home. And once you experience the home spa lifestyle, you'll wonder how you ever lived without it.

Hot Tubs

1 Getting into Hot Tubs

Like many people, I learn best by getting my hands dirty. Book smarts are one thing, but nothing beats practical experience. In between, however, is that foolhardy stage where there's neither scholarly credits nor useful skills to fall back on. After these scrape-by-by-the-skin-of-our-teeth moments, we often hear ourselves say things like "Next time I'll do it differently" or "If I only knew then what I know now."

◀ A sturdy arbor shades this spa, which is partially recessed in the ground and surrounded on two sides by a privacy wall.

When purchasing my first house, I didn't know enough about residential construction to build a birdhouse. But that didn't stop me from embarking upon that adventure. And I can say similar things about my early efforts at vegetable gardening, computer repair, and surfing.

Of course, I know now how valuable some good books on these subjects would have been (though I wonder whether my ego would have allowed me to read them at the time). Nevertheless, I encourage you to gather all of the information you can before installing your own hot tub. My spa is conveniently located on ground level off the master bedroom, and a bluestone path connects the house to the steamy oasis. During the summer it's surrounded by colorful honeysuckle and clematis that cling to a louvered privacy fence I built myself. And in the winter the spa provides a spectacular view of the starry sky. Even so, I can't help imagining how it all might be a bit better if some things had been done differently.

This section is intended to inspire and prepare you to build the hot tub environment of your dreams. If you follow this advice, I guarantee that you'll eliminate most of your could've-would've-should've.

SPA HISTORY AND CONTEMPORARY TRENDS

For thousands of years, people from nearly every continent have been drawn to the therapeutic wonders of hot water. The Greeks and Romans may be best known for their bathing rituals because of the massive and magnificent baths they built — some large enough to cater to thousands of bathers at a time. However, other civilizations also have a history steeped in bathing traditions.

The Roman baths were a place where all of society could recreate and relax. On the

▲ Hot-water bathing continues to be an integral part of many cultures. In Japan, for example, the *ofuro* is not only a way to cleanse the body, but also a means of improving one's mental, physical, and spiritual health.

other end of the spectrum is the centuries-old Japanese *ofuro*, traditionally a freestanding wooden tub for individual hot-water bathing. The *ofuro* is as much a part of Japanese culture as are the better-known exports sushi and karaoke. More than just a way to wash away the day's dirt and grime, an *ofuro* incorporates botanicals, minerals, and herbal extracts that enhance the therapeutic benefits of bathing — mental, physical, and spiritual.

Native Americans engaged in a culture of hot-water bathing, too. Instead of a wooden tub, however, they simply dipped into natural hot springs, which were believed to have therapeutic properties. For hundreds of years, people have sought out natural hot springs for their alleged curative powers. Today many of these hot springs have been fashioned into resort spas.

The hot tub as we know it today, however, originated in the 1960s. During this period wooden bathtubs were created from old oak barrels and vats used for winemaking in California. Early prototypes were reminiscent of the Japanese *ofuro*. As manufacturing processes were developed, most wooden hot tubs were made from regional redwood. As the product developed, circulating pumps and heaters were added to keep the water temperature high. But let's face it, a wooden tub sitting in the harsh elements of nature can easily develop leaks and play host to a variety of unhealthy bacteria.

Which brings us to the modern-day hot tub or spa. Though many lavish hot tubs are constructed using the same materials and techniques used to build concrete swimming pools, the vast majority of hot tubs are prefabricated in factories using acrylic shells surrounded by wooden or synthetic skirts. The shells are molded to fit the human form, and powerful jet action provides hydrotherapy. With factory-installed plumbing and filtration systems, the units are relatively easy to install. It's just a matter of choosing the one that has the amenities you and your family are seeking.

Before we move on any further, now I'd like to clarify some terminology. When manufacturers started to build hot tubs from colorful acrylic sheets, the results were a smooth, luxurious, and attractive surface. To separate this new class of products from the traditional wooden hot tub, companies began referring to their products as spas. But old habits are hard to break. Industry research has shown that most consumers refer to a freestanding, jetted tub of water as a hot tub, regardless of its composition and form. Plus, the tremendous growth in the resort spa industry has caused most people to think of massages, facials, and seaweed wraps when they hear the word *spa*. Still, many hot tub dealers and manufacturers have kept the word in their names. So now when someone says, "I'm going to Spa Dreams this afternoon," you're not sure whether she's checking out hot tubs or getting a pedicure.

For the purposes of this book, I use the terms *hot tub* and *spa* interchangeably for variety's sake and because this book is about creating a resort spa environment in your own home with spas, saunas, and steam baths.

Now that that's settled, there's one more issue of semantics that needs to be clarified: the use of the word *Jacuzzi*. Jacuzzi is a trademarked brand name of jetted bathtubs and spas and should not be used when talking about hot tubs or spas generically. Undoubtedly, this issue alone has kept the company's legal department busy for years. It's like trying to get people to refer to a generic box of facial tissue as tissue after they've been referring to it as Kleenex their whole lives.

Since I've opened up a proverbial can of worms by mentioning jetted bathtubs, I'm compelled to make some editorial remarks. Although progress has been made to make jetted bathtubs more like hot tubs, they aren't. And those who say the bathing experiences are the same are . . . well, let me put it this way. Do you recall when in the 1998 vice presidential debates, Dan Quayle compared the length of his service in Congress with John F. Kennedy's? Technically, it was true, but it prompted his opponent, the Democrat Lloyd Bentsen, to say: "I served with Jack Kennedy. I knew Jack Kennedy. Jack Kennedy was a friend of mine. Senator, you are no Jack Kennedy."

Ouch!

Yet I'd second that stinging rebuke for anyone who tried to imply that a jetted bathtub has the therapeutic benefits equal to those of a hot tub: "I've relaxed in hot tubs. I know hot tubs. Hot tubs are a necessity of

▲ A simple spa fits snugly on this wooden deck, where bathers can enjoy the ocean view. Before installing a spa on a deck, make sure that the deck is designed to accomodate the weight of the spa — including the water and the bathers.

mine. Jetted bath, you are no hot tub." Most jetted baths aren't as deep as hot tubs, nor do they provide sufficient jet action. Unlike hot tubs, most jetted baths must be drained after each use because they don't have a system for filtering or sanitizing the water. Plus, they are rarely big enough for more than one adult to comfortably bathe. Where's the party in that?

Like I said, technological advances are occurring, and it won't be many years before the jetted tub is revolutionized to compete more directly with hot tubs. Until that day, however, this section of the book deals solely with hot tubs . . . er . . . um . . . or spas.

What's in It for You

Whether it's a quiet soak or a vigorous massage you seek, the soothing effects of hot tub therapy can't be duplicated. The massaging action of warm water reduces muscle soreness and stiffness and eases the pain of arthritis. In fact, the Arthritis Foundation recommends hot-water therapy for relief of arthritis pain. In addition, the heat causes blood vessels to dilate, which lowers blood pressure. And the buoyancy of the water greatly reduces the workload on your heart and muscles. Some people credit spas with reducing stress, promoting more restful sleep, mimicking the benefits of exercise for people with type 2 diabetes, and ridding the body of toxins by encouraging sweating.

As research into hot-water therapy continues, the list of benefits continues to grow. But not as quickly as the styles and options available to today's consumers. Indeed, spas can be as basic as white boxers or as luxurious as silk pajamas. While shopping for the perfect spa, don't be surprised when you encounter a litany of hot tub amenities that have little to do with hydrotherapy and everything to do with making the spa experience more enticing. Be on the lookout for:

- LED underwater lights that change colors

- Fiber-optic accent lights around the spa

- CD/stereo systems with waterproof speakers

- Waterfalls and misters

- Built-in cup holders and ice buckets

- Integrated aromatherapy systems

- Built-in TV screens

- Computer terminals networked to the Internet

With so many options, it's easy to see why choosing the right hot tub can be a daunting, and often frustrating, task. You can spend countless hours surfing the Internet and visiting spa dealers, but the information overload can leave you more confused than before you started. My advice: Take a deep breath, consider how you're going to use your spa so that you don't pay for superfluous amenities, and stay focused on comfort and hydrotherapy.

To that end, it helps to know a bit about the construction and operation of a hot tub, which can be easily understood if you look at it piece by piece.

INNER WORKINGS

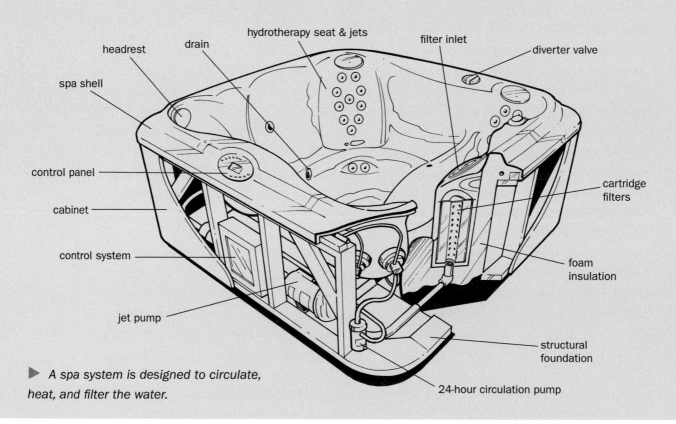

▶ *A spa system is designed to circulate, heat, and filter the water.*

CHOOSING THE RIGHT SPA

Purchasing a spa or hot tub is an extremely personal affair, like selecting an automobile or ordering a specialty coffee. One person's nirvana is another person's nightmare. Yet all spas have a few things in common, and knowing what those are will come in handy when it's time to comparison shop.

Essentially, every spa is composed of a shell that holds water, a cabinet that surrounds the shell, some jets that provide hydrotherapy, a circulating system that pumps and filters the water, and some controls that make the whole thing work. As with owning a car, you don't need to know how every component is manufactured, but it helps to know the steering wheel from the stereo and the tires from the transmission. So here's a quick rundown of the major spa components you should be familiar with if you plan to own one.

The Shell

When you look at a spa, the first thing you notice is the shell, the vessel that holds the water. Though you can still find traditional hot tubs made from wood, most of today's prefabricated spas are made from acrylic, thermoplastic, fiberglass, tile, or soft vinyl. Custom concrete spas are also popular and can be installed alone or in combination with a swimming pool. If your vision for a spa environment simply doesn't mesh with any of the prefabricated spas on the market, you'll have to look at custom spa construction, which is likely to carry a price tag double or triple the cost of a prefabricated version.

By far, the most popular material for factory-made spas is acrylic, which comes in an array of appealing colors, from midnight blue to Caribbean sand. Acrylic also comes in several surface styles, from smooth, glossy finishes that resemble shiny new automobiles to faux granite surfaces that make the spa look as though it's been carved from stone. This vast selection of colors and styles makes it possible to find a spa that perfectly complements your indoor or outdoor decor.

The acrylic sheets used to form spa shells are differentiated by their thickness, the way they are backed for structural support, and the method used in forming them into spa shells. Most spa manufacturers use a single acrylic sheet and reinforce it with a layer of fiberglass or thermoplastic. Only a few

▲ A cover lift makes it easy to manuever heavy or awkward spa covers. Spa steps are used for easy entry.

companies supply acrylic sheeting to the spa industry, which is why spas from two different spa manufacturers may look similar.

So what truly differentiates one acrylic spa shell from another? Simply put, it's the seating configuration. Hot tubs are designed to accommodate anywhere from one to more than ten bathers, although the average seating capacity is five or six adults. Among these sizes you'll find a vast array of seating configurations using various combinations of lounges, bucket seats, and benches.

To determine the shell configuration that is right for you, think about how you plan to use your spa. On the one hand, if you're imagining intimate, moonlit soaks with a significant other, you might want a small two-person spa with dual lounges. On the other hand, if you're dreaming of wild hot tub parties with your posse of friends, then you'll want as much seating room as possible. And if your spa is going indoors, you'll want to restrict your choices to models that will fit through your doorways.

Meanwhile, don't overlook the growing trend of fitness spas and swim spas, which provide warm-water therapy and enough space for a cardiovascular and strength-training workout. A fitness spa incorporates resistance equipment for strength training, and a swim spa is equipped with a powerful swim jet that creates an adjustable current that you can swim against. (For more information, see Swim & Fitness Spas, page 16).

SIZE MATTERS

Whether you're looking for an intimate spa for two or a party spa for ten, there's a spa design out there for you. By finding the right combination of bucket seats, cool-down benches, and lounges, you'll have an ideal spa that meets all of your therapeutic and entertainment needs.

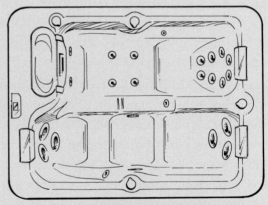
Two-person spa with dual lounges.

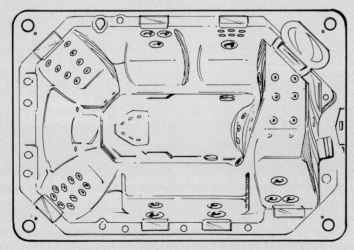
Eight-person spa with bucket, bench, and lounge seating.

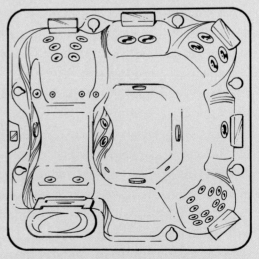
Six-person spa with a variety of seating options.

As you search for that perfect spa shell design, don't underestimate the importance of comfort. You'll be using your new spa for many years, so you'll want one that you find relaxing. Good spa retailers will encourage you to sit in the dry spas they have on display. And an increasing number of dealers are creating private "mood rooms" where shoppers can don bathing suits and try out operational spas before they buy. This way you can truly see how comfortable the spa is when it's filled with water, whether the water is deep enough for your liking, and whether there's adequate room to stretch out and do those aquatic exercises you like. Most people wouldn't dream of buying a car without taking it for a test drive, so why buy a spa before taking it for a test soak?

The Cabinet

Another highly visible part of the hot tub is the cabinet that encloses the shell and all of the plumbing and equipment. Traditionally, spa manufacturers have made spa skirts out of redwood or cedar, both of which look beautiful when new but require annual refinishing to maintain their luster — more often if the wood is exposed to direct sunlight. Also, wood eventually weakens and succumbs to the elements, especially if a spa cover removal device is attached to the cabinet, which puts extra strain on the wood.

To offer more durable and maintenance-free cabinets, some manufacturers have begun using simulated wood made of polymers. An embossed wood grain and warm coloring give some of these faux wood skirts a natural appearance. Best of all, the polymer material is maintenance-free and often comes with a manufacturer's warranty. A few spa models eliminate the wood skirts entirely by making the cabinet out of the same acrylic used to form the spa shell. A cabinet that

▲ Synthetic spa skirts offer the durability of plastic with the look of wood, stone, or other natural material.

matches the shell can give a uniform appearance to a spa installation and is a nice option if you don't like the look of wood.

The Jets

While the spa shell is important for reasons of aesthetics and comfort, the hydrotherapy jets deserve equal, if not more, attention. Spa jets have the power to transform an oversize tub of stagnant water into a therapeutic oasis that rejuvenates the mind, body, and spirit.

Jets come in many styles, and new ones are being introduced every year, so you'll want to look carefully at the types of jets a spa has before making a purchase. Some popular jet types include neck jets, foot jets, stationery jets, cluster jets, oscillating or rotating jets, directional jets, whirlpool jets, and handheld jets. If a spa model that you like doesn't have a jet configuration that meets your needs, you might be able to have the spa customized with the kind of jets you want. Ask your dealer.

A few other things to consider about jets:

● *Don't choose quantity over quality.* As a new spa buyer, it's easy to be wooed by the number of spa jets a particular model boasts. However, pay attention to the types of jets that are included and where they are placed. For example, a single jet perfectly placed to provide the lower back pain relief you're seeking is worth a dozen jets that hit you in the wrong places.

● *Take a wet test.* The surest way to make sure a spa's jets are providing the hydrotherapy you want is to try it out. Better dealers provide private, comfortable rooms just for this purpose.

● *Don't forget the aerator.* The typical spa comes equipped with a blower or aerator that allows you to control the amount of air that is mixed with the water streaming from the jets. The more air you introduce, the more powerful the jet action. Experiment with this feature so that you can experience the full range of hydrotherapy a particular jet or cluster of jets provides.

With the right jet configuration, you won't want to leave your tub. On the flip side, the wrong jet configuration — even with comfortable, ergonomically styled seating — won't provide a satisfactory hydro-massage. So explore your options and shop wisely.

The Pump

One of the greatest mistakes people make with spa pumps is assuming that bigger is better. Dealers often promote bigger pumps as evidence of the quality of their spas. In fact, a pump that is oversized can wreak havoc on a spa's plumbing system and waste energy to boot. With a prefabricated spa, the manufacturer has already sized the pump that comes with the spa to work at maximum efficiency for that particular spa model. Trouble can arise, however, when a pump needs to be replaced and the spa owner thinks he or she should get a more powerful pump to make the jet action stronger.

When purchasing a replacement pump, note that there are two ways to rate a pump's horsepower: start-up horsepower and continuous operating horsepower. Make sure you're comparing apples to apples when you go shopping and that you select the size of pump recommended by the spa's manufacturer. The start-up horsepower is the power required to initially start the pump. It takes less power to keep the pump running, and this is called continuous operating horsepower. A pump rated 3 hp at start-up may not run as strongly as a pump rated 3 hp for continuous operation.

▲ Today's spas engage all of the senses. Not only is this integrated fountain interesting to look at, but it also creates a pleasing sound when the other jets are turned off.

HYDROTHERAPY

Jets should target key body parts to produce the greatest hydrotherapy effects. More is not necessarily better if they don't produce the massaging action you want.

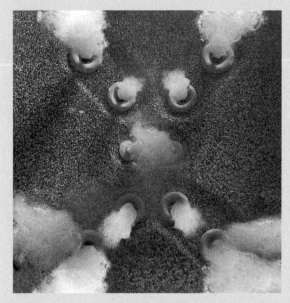

Air mixes with water to increase the intensity of the jet action.

Large, rotating jets target the back while smaller jets zero in on shoulder muscles.

Strategically placed jets target major back muscles, the outer thighs, and the calves.

Powerful floor jets massage the feet.

SWIM & FITNESS SPAS

Aquatic exercise has always been promoted as a healthful fitness activity, especially for those with weak joints or who are overweight. An estimated six million people currently take part in some form of aquatic exercise other than swimming. Rehab centers have long used aquatic therapy to speed the recovery process after surgery, and the Arthritis Foundation has offered a warm-water aquatic exercise program for years. "Water is a safe, ideal environment for relieving arthritis pain and stiffness," the organization says. "Water exercise is especially good for people with arthritis because it allows you to exercise without putting excess strain on your joints and muscles."

To take advantage of aquatic exercise in the comfort of your own home, you may want to consider a swim spa or fitness spa. Swim spas are large, deep spas with a swim jet on one end that creates a continuous current for users to swim against. The current can be dialed up or down to customize the workout. Fitness spas may have a swim jet, but they also incorporate exercise equipment for stretching and strength training. And when you're finished with your workout, you can relax in the spa's built-in seating, which includes hydrotherapy jets.

Originally marketed toward baby boomers who want aerobic exercise and strength training, fitness spas really offer something for the entire family. Indeed, with the growing popularity of water aerobics and aquatic exercise, an array of related products and accessories has made its way into the market. In other words, there's no need to get bored doing the same exercises over and over again. Here is a sampling of products that can help you vary your warm-water workouts so you stay motivated to exercise:

- *Aqua gloves,* which have webbing between the fingers for greater resistance

- *Aqua shoes,* for better traction when water walking

- *Aqua weights,* which attach to your waist, ankles, and wrists for strength training

- *Kickboards,* which support your upper body while you are exercising your legs

- *Balance boards,* which enable swimmers to stand, sit, or kneel with their heads out of the water while they perform dynamic movements with the arms, legs, and waist

- *Inflatable collars and pillows,* which help swimmers float on their backs while exercising

- *Exercise balls* for stretching, resistance training, and improving hand-eye coordination

- *Flotation devices* (such as belts and water noodles) for added buoyancy, especially during aqua jogging

- *Resistance devices* such as arm and leg splints, paddles, fins, and bands

- *Underwater steps,* for aerobic exercise and strength training

- *Underwater treadmills*

- *Floating barbells* for strength training

Most of these products are available through pool and spa supply retailers, online retailers, or catalogs, such as Sprint Aquatics.

For those concerned about keeping such a large spa (two thousand to three thousand gallons or 7.6 to 11.4 kiloliters) heated, don't worry. Like a traditional spa, a fitness spa is fully insulated and has a cover that traps in heat when the spa is not in use.

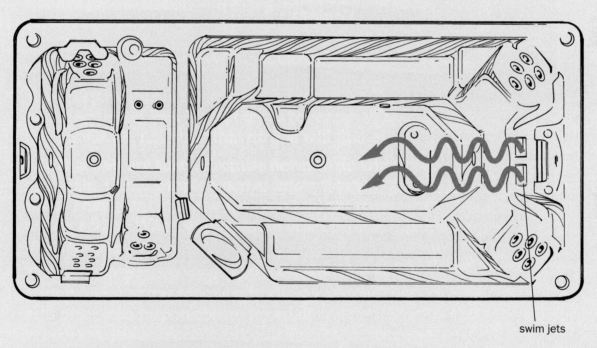

swim jets

▲ *A swim or exercise spa allows you to swim against a current of water or to use aquatic exercise equipment in the large area. The small area holds warmer water and provides the hydrotherapy of a traditional hot tub.*

Also note the number of pumps your spa has and to which tasks each pump is assigned. For example, some units have a two-speed pump: The low speed is used for mild jet action and for circulating the water during the filtration cycles, and the high speed is for greater hydrotherapy. Other spas have a 24-hour circulation pump that routes the water through purifying equipment and the heater, thereby allowing the main pump to focus on the single task of providing jet action.

If your spa does not have a small continuous-recirculation pump for heating and sanitizing the water, these tasks will need to be done by the hydrotherapy pump, which will come on during routine filtration cycles. This large pump is more expensive to operate than the small one, and it will need to run longer than it otherwise would to achieve the proper temperature and sanitizer levels.

Also note that each hydrotherapy pump supplies water to specific jets. Make sure you're getting what you expect. For example, the jets in the bucket seat you love might not be paired with the powerful two-speed pump you dream about.

Typically, the more jets you have, the more pumps you'll need to supply water to the jets. It's common for spa pumps to supply water to two or more sets of jets. In such cases you'll need to operate a diverter valve to send the water where you want it — for example, away from your feet and toward a bucket seat in the opposite corner.

The Heater

The most vulnerable piece of spa equipment is the electric heater. That's because the heating elements come in contact with the spa water, which can be very corrosive. Over time the heater can fail. (The best thing you can do to prolong your heater's life is to keep your spa water properly balanced. This prevents the water from becoming overly corrosive. For more on water chemistry, see the section on maintaining your spa, page 38.)

Several spa manufacturers have addressed the problem of heater failure by switching to heaters that don't allow water to touch the heating elements. Instead, the elements are wrapped around stainless-steel tubes that the water flows through. These heaters can drive up the cost of a spa, but they last longer than traditional spa heaters. They can also increase operational costs, because only about 60 percent of the heat generated is transferred to the water, whereas the immersion-style heaters transfer 100 percent of their heat to the water.

Most spa heaters are designed to heat the water to a maximum recommended temperature of 104°F (40°C). Temperatures above that may cause bathers to pass out. Most people find a temperature range of 100 to 103°F (38 to 39°C) to be most comfortable.

Most spa heaters have a 5- to 6-kilowatt capacity, which should be enough to maintain the desired spa temperature, even with the spa's insulating cover removed. However, if you live in a colder climate, check with the spa dealer to make sure the heater for the spa you're considering is powerful enough to heat the water during the winter months.

The Filter

The filter screens fine particles and debris out of the spa water. Concrete spas built in conjunction with swimming pools often share the pool's filtration system, which could be a sand filter, a diatomaceous earth filter, or a cartridge filter. Prefabricated stand-alone spas typically use cartridge filters to screen particles out of the water and keep it sparkling clear. Cartridge filters are cylindrical and contain pleated fabric that's

SPA POWER

Energy conservation continues to be of great concern for many people. With the unpredictability of energy prices in many regions, it's wise to be concerned about the energy your new spa will consume. How much a spa costs to operate depends on several factors:

- *The model and size you select*

- *The temperature you want*

- *How frequently you use the spa*

- *The air temperature outside the spa*

- *The cost of energy in your area*

Hot tubs, especially those installed outdoors, have a reputation for squandering energy, but new technology and manufacturing techniques have made spas more energy-efficient than you may think. A typical four- or five-person spa costs just $10 to $12 per month to heat, based on $.07/kW hour, a set temperature of 102 to 104°F (39 to 40°C), and approximately 12 to 15 hours of usage during the month (or about 30 to 45 minutes every other day). One industry study shows that the average spa costs about $20 per month to heat. Either way, it's rather affordable.

A spa dealer should be able to help you estimate the energy cost of a particular spa in your area. The best way to conserve energy, however, is to buy a spa that's well insulated. Better-insulated spas use closed-cell polyurethane foam, the same material used in freezers, as insulation. Also, make sure your spa includes an insulated cover that forms a tight seal around spa's lip.

You can also conserve energy by reducing the temperature of the water during nonuse times, shortening the length of filtration cycles (assuming the water quality isn't compromised), and installing the spa in a sheltered area away from wind.

---

supported by a core and two end caps. Some spas require one large cartridge filter, while others may require several smaller ones.

Not all cartridge filters are created equal. Some contain more filtering material than others do. Here again, however, bigger is not always better. A cartridge filter needs to be sized with the entire circulation system in mind to ensure that proper filtration occurs. Typically, the square footage of filter media is matched with the gallon-per-minute flow of the pumps. If there is too much pump for the filter media, unfiltered water can be forced back into the spa. If there isn't enough pump for the filter media, the jet action can be reduced. Manufacturers' guidelines will tell you which size filter is right for your spa.

Cartridge filters need to be cleaned every few months or whenever the flow rate of water seems restricted. Cleaning a cartridge filter is simply a matter of removing it from the filter bay and hosing it off with a garden hose, being sure to focus on the deep recesses of the pleats, where dirt accumulates. For more information on cleaning cartridge filters, see page 53.

THREE WAYS TO CONVENIENTLY CONTROL YOUR SPA

Monitoring your outdoor spa from inside your home is easy with remote-control technology. You can check the water temperature, fire up the heater, or turn on lights and pumps without making a trip out to the hot tub. For additional convenience, some spa manufacturers offer waterproof handheld remote controls that can be used in the tub.

Hardwired System
Data travels via low-voltage wires

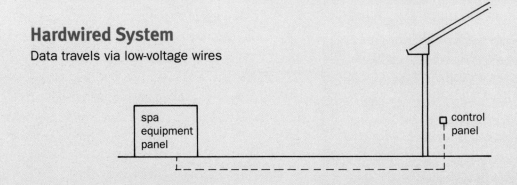

Radio Frequency System
Data travels via radio waves

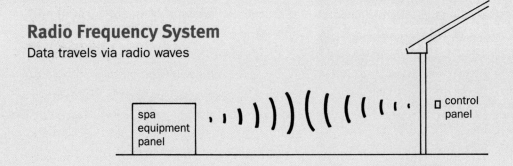

Power Line Carrier System
Data travels via the home's electrical system

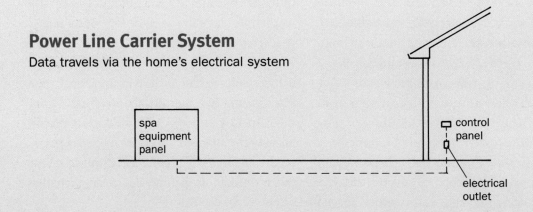

The Controls

Spa controls typically enable you to set the water temperature, turn lights on and off, power up the pumps and blower, see whether ancillary equipment is operating, and lock the controls so no one can change the temperature or operate the pump while you're away. They come bundled with a prefabricated spa, and you won't have any choice in which type the manufacturer uses. With a custom spa, however, you may get to choose your controls. Either way, test whether their operation makes sense to you.

Most spa controls are preprogrammed to run the filtration cycle for at least 30 minutes four times a day, but you'll want to customize the time and duration of the cycle to meet your spa's filtration needs. For example, a spa used by two people for several hours a week will require less filtration than the same spa used by six bathers for a couple hours every day. Of course, you could "overfilter" your spa just to be on the safe side, but this wastes energy. Trial and error will help you settle on the perfect filtration cycle for you. For more information on saving energy costs, see Spa Power, page 19.

For convenience, many spa manufacturers install dual controls: a main control panel at the front of the spa and secondary controls on the opposite side for ease in operating the jets. Handheld remote controls are growing in popularity, and more spa owners are opting to have auxiliary control panels installed in their homes so they don't have to trek out to the spa to check the water temperature, fire up the jets, or turn on the lights.

Some automated spa controls are accessible via telephone, so you can turn on the heater while you're stuck in rush-hour traffic. And be on the lookout for computerized monitoring systems that enable you to check on your spa via the Internet — a great feature if your spa is located at a vacation home you visit only on weekends.

Other Considerations

Other considerations will influence the type of spa you purchase, including your confidence in the dealer, the selection in your area, and the manufacturer's warranty. Another key consideration is the design of your spa environment, including whether the hot tub will be placed outside on a concrete slab, recessed beneath a wooden deck, or in a sunroom off the master bedroom. Indeed, the design of your spa environment will dictate which spas you can choose from. So before you go shopping, be sure to read the next section on planning the ultimate spa setting.

PLANNING AND DESIGNING THE SPA ENVIRONMENT

Installing a spa can be as simple as placing the unit on a structurally sound deck or as elaborate as recessing it in the ground and surrounding it with stone pavers and lush plantings. You can place it in a solarium or make it part of a home gym. The type of installation you choose depends on the type of spa environment you want to create and the size of your budget.

Before settling on an installation site, consider whether there's adequate access for your spa to reach its final destination. Is the pathway wide and tall enough? Are there any obstacles that need to be moved? Should any tree branches be cut back? Are gates wide enough for the spa to fit through? In some instances, it may be necessary to hire a crane operator to lift the spa over the house and lower it into place in the backyard. Most dealers are prepared for this, and the extra cost to you should be no more than a few hundred dollars, depending on how far the crane must travel.

◀ Partially recessing a spa in a wooden deck makes it easier to access from all sides. This spa, complete with retractable waterproof speakers, is flanked on two sides by deck benches, enabling nonbathers and bathers alike to enjoy the hot tub setting.

Also, the vast majority of spas need to be hardwired to a 220-volt electrical source equipped with a GFCI (ground fault circuit interrupter). So make sure your electrician is able to bring power to where you intend to place your hot tub.

Here is a look at the most popular types of spa installations to consider: wooden deck, patio deck, in-ground, and indoors.

Wooden Deck Installations

Wooden decks are a popular location for spas because they provide easy access to and from the home. Before you place a spa on your deck, however, make sure it can support the weight of the spa (including that of the water and a maximum number of bathers). The weight of the spa, when full, is usually supplied in the owner's manual. You'll have to estimate the weight of bathers on your own.

Once you know the maximum weight to expect, check with a building contractor or engineer to see whether your deck can handle the load or will require additional structural support. If you're building a new deck, alert your deck builder to your plans for a spa so that he or she can design a deck to suit your needs. You may want to consider erecting a privacy screen as part of the deck to add intimacy to your spa area and to block the wind.

If your deck is raised high enough above the ground, you might consider recessing the spa beneath the deck for an "in-ground" look. Typically, this calls for building a steel-reinforced concrete pad beneath the deck for the spa to sit on and then building the deck around the spa so that just the lip rises above the deck. Another option is to partially recess the spa into the decking and build steps around the spa that can double as bench seating.

Whatever you plan, be sure to leave room for removing and storing the cover when the spa is in use.

ALL CLEAR

Before you write that check, be sure you can get the spa where you want it. Hot tubs are large, cumbersome objects. They might call them "portable spas," but there isn't much that is "portable" about them. To ensure an easy delivery, make sure that all obstacles have been cleared.

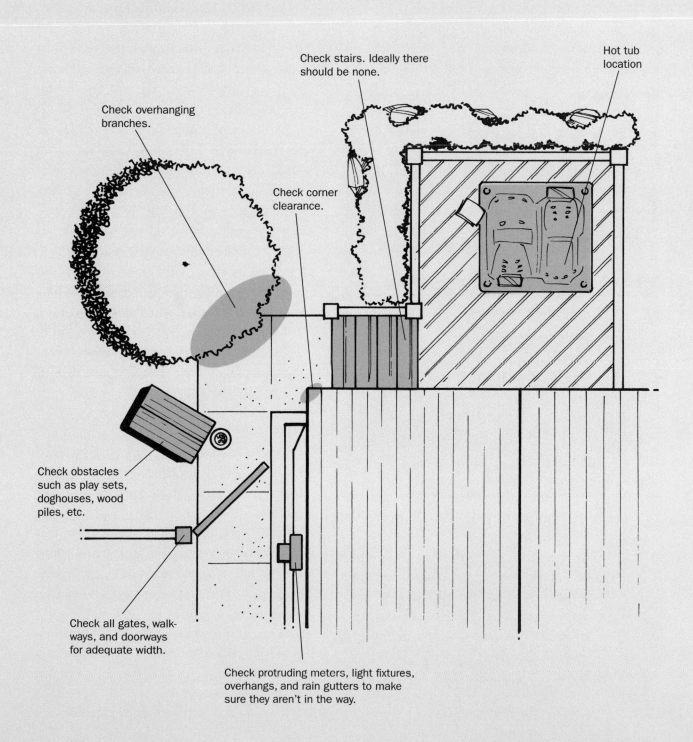

Check stairs. Ideally there should be none.

Hot tub location

Check overhanging branches.

Check corner clearance.

Check obstacles such as play sets, doghouses, wood piles, etc.

Check all gates, walkways, and doorways for adequate width.

Check protruding meters, light fixtures, overhangs, and rain gutters to make sure they aren't in the way.

INSTALLATION INSIGHTS

Options abound for designing your spa environment. Indoors or outdoors? On the deck or in the ground? It's important to know your options before planning your hot tub installation. For example, wooden decks must be structurally sound to hold the spa's weight, patio decks must drain away from the spa, and indoor rooms must have adequate ventilation. Looks, style, convenience, and cost will all play a role in your decision.

Wooden deck, atop

Patio, partially recessed

Wooden deck, fully recessed

Patio Deck Installations

If your spa is being placed on the ground, it must sit on a level, solid foundation. Otherwise, the spa could become damaged, and most warranties are void if the product isn't installed properly. One of the best foundations is a reinforced concrete pad at least 4 inches (10 cm) thick. Some other materials you might be able to use to create a solid foundation are bricks or railroad ties. Just make sure that the surface is stable and won't sink in spots, which could cause the spa to become unleveled.

Colored and stamped concrete, which can be designed to look like a wide variety of bricks and stones, is an increasingly popular choice for patios. Though more expensive than traditional concrete patios, stamped concrete patios are often less costly than real stone patios and are easier to maintain.

When locating your spa on a patio, consider how convenient it is to the house, how much privacy you'll have from the neighbors, and how easy it will be to move around it. The cabinet door should be accessible in case equipment repairs need to be made, so position the spa accordingly.

In-Ground Installations

Concrete in-ground spas can be installed independently from or in conjunction with in-ground pools. Many spa and pool combinations feature an elevated spa that spills into the pool, thereby creating a water feature that's both inviting to look at and soothing to listen to. These spas are usually surfaced with the same material — plaster, stone aggregate, or tile — used in the pool.

Some homeowners opt to install prefabricated acrylic or fiberglass spas alongside their concrete pools because of the better seating configurations and hydrotherapy they offer. If your prefabricated spa is being installed below grade, your builder should create a vault, often lined with concrete, to hold your tub. A sump pump or draining system should be included in the vault if there's a possibility of water accumulating in the vault and coming in contact with the spa's electrical equipment.

As with a recessed installation on a wooden deck, the lip of the spa should remain above grade to prevent rainwater from running into the tub and to ensure a tight seal between the spa and the insulating cover. The surrounding deck, meanwhile, can run the gamut from patterned concrete to brick pavers to cut flagstone. You might even consider dressing up the area with an outdoor fire pit (gas or wood), outdoor kitchen, and outdoor shower. After all, this is your spa environment, so make it as simple or as luxurious as you want (or can afford).

Indoor Installations

The best part of owning an indoor spa is that you can always enjoy a relaxing soak no matter what the weather is doing outside. Plus, you can place your spa in a sunroom or solarium, helping to create the illusion of being outside. And depending on the type of installation you're doing, you still have the option of having the spa sit on the floor or rest below grade.

However, don't assume that an indoor spa is simply a hot tub in a room with four walls and a roof. Indoor spas present a litany of problems never encountered with an outside installation. The biggest challenge will be making sure there's adequate heating and ventilation to prevent excessive humidity, which can cause structural damage to the home. A hot tub gives off a lot of steam, which can damage unprotected woodwork

RECESSING YOUR HOT TUB INTO A WOODEN DECK

A spa that is recessed into a wooden deck can be easier to enter and exit, and it doesn't block backyard views like a spa that is placed atop a deck. When building this type of installation, you need to create a 4-inch (10 cm) steel-reinforced concrete pad to support the weight of the spa. You'll also need to make sure that the spa equipment is accessible for repairs and maintenance.

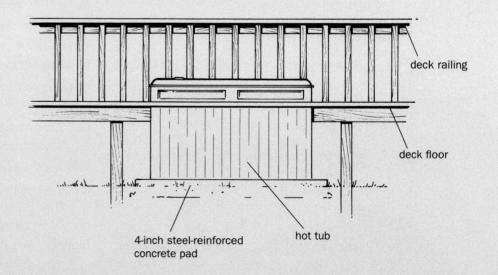

deck railing

deck floor

4-inch steel-reinforced concrete pad

hot tub

▲ Expansive windows bring the outdoors into this hot tub solarium. Tile flooring is an ideal surface for any indoor spa installation.

and may produce dry rot, mildew, mold, and other problems.

Check with an architect and HVAC (heating, ventilation, and air-conditioning) specialist to ensure that the spa room has enough ventilation and is equipped to prevent moisture damage. Of course, every situation is different, and several factors contribute to how quickly water evaporates from an indoor spa:

- *The relative humidity of the room*

- *The surface area of the water*

- *The temperature of the water*

- *The temperature of the air*

- *How long the cover stays off the spa*

- *How much splashing occurs from bathers, jets, and water features*

The larger the spa, the greater the evaporation. Evaporation also increases when the water is warmer than the air and there's lots of water being splashed out of the tub. Briefly stated, when water evaporates, it causes the water temperature to drop, the air temperature to increase, and the room's humidity level to rise. The resulting warm, moist conditions are a veritable paradise for mold and mildew. If there's any aspect of your spa installation that you're trying to cut corners on in order to reduce costs, you don't want it to be in the area of air quality. In fact, health research has shown that poorly ventilated indoor pool and spa environments can cause respiratory problems when aerosolized water particles carrying bacteria are allowed to enter the lungs. The medical term for this is *hypersensitivity pneumonitis.* Fortunately, this needn't be a concern if you have adequate dehumidification and air exchange, and if you cover your spa whenever it's not in use. For more information on preventing hypersensitivity pneumonitis with indoor spas, see page 52.

ASK YOURSELF...

To help you get the most pleasure from your spa investment, ask yourself these questions.

1 **HOW DO I PLAN TO USE MY SPA?** Here are some possible answers: entertaining, family gatherings, relaxation, exercise, or all of the above. Answering this question will help you focus on the type of spa and accessories that will suit your needs.

2 **WHAT OTHER HOBBIES DO I ENJOY?** Your answers may run the gamut, from working out to listening to music. Either way, you'll know whether you'll get more enjoyment from a fitness spa or one with a built-in CD player.

3 **HOW CAN I ENGAGE MORE OF MY SENSES?** This might lead you to choose spa fragrances, a built-in refrigerator, colored underwater lights, waterproof speakers, water features and misters, or cozy spa-side furniture.

4 **WHAT CAN I DO TO REDUCE MAINTENANCE?** This could lead you toward automatic sanitizers, more efficient filtration equipment, and specialty chemicals.

5 **HOW CAN I GET MORE USE OUT OF MY SPA?** The answer might prompt you to purchase, among other options, a cover removal device that makes the spa easier to access or landscape lighting that makes nighttime use more inviting.

Indoor spas do require a lot of planning and design to ensure that the finished room has good air quality, adequate drainage, durable construction, and safe lighting. Following are some things to consider.

Dehumidifiers and Air-Exchange Systems. Because room and spa sizes differ greatly, dehumidifiers are sized individually for each installation. Most of them work best when the water is 2 to 4 degrees Fahrenheit (one to two degrees Celsius) warmer than the air. But that's not likely to be the case when your hot tub is 104°F (40°C) and your room temperature is normally 72°F (22°C). That's why it's important to have a dehumidifier that can handle the high rate of evaporation and to keep the spa covered when it's not being used. Consult an HVAC contractor experienced with indoor pool installations to make sure the unit you buy can handle the volume of air and humidity levels expected.

While a dehumidifier will attack the moisture in the air, nothing improves air quality better than an air-exchange system that brings a fresh supply of air into the room at all times. In some cases the air-exchange system may be part of a dehumidification system that simply exchanges the moist inside air with drier fresh air from outside.

In addition to improving air quality, an air-exchange system can be used to keep windows and glass doors from fogging up. This is accomplished by installing vents along the floor across the entire width of the windows. The effect is the same as when you turn on your car's ventilation system to clear up a fogged windshield. If the room has floor-to-ceiling windows or sliding glass doors, you may need to install vents in both the floor and the ceiling to ensure clear panes. This is where an experienced HVAC contractor is invaluable. He or she will be able to assess your situation and design a system that removes moist air before it has a chance to cause structural damage. You can search for an HVAC contractor in the telephone directory, but it's typically better to get a recommendation from a home builder or pool builder who has worked on indoor pools before.

Spa water that is properly balanced and sanitized shouldn't have a strong chemical odor. Nevertheless, a good air-exchange system will keep any smells to a minimum.

Vapor Barriers. Depending on the materials used to build your indoor spa room, you may need to use a vapor barrier — typically thick sheets of overlapping plastic that separate the structural framework and insulation from the drywall. This will prevent moisture from reaching the structural framework, where it can foster mold or cause freeze/thaw damage. For the walls themselves, some builders believe that greenboard, a water-resistant drywall often used in bathrooms, is sufficient. Others recommend a waterproof concrete board, such as WonderBoard. Still others recommend Dryvit, a material designed for exterior applications that is available in several textures and finishes. Of course, tile, stone, glass block, and other masonry items are well suited for wet spa areas. Your builder or architect can help you decide which materials are best suited for your application.

Floors and Floor Drains. Before placing a spa indoors, make sure that the floor is structurally sound and can support the weight of the spa plus the weight of the water and the bathers. Water will accumulate around the tub, so the floor coverings should be nonslip and a floor drain should be installed. The drain also makes it easy to drain the spa when it's time to change the water. Of course, it's also handy to have a water spigot and hose nearby for refilling the tub.

▲ Reminiscent of the Roman baths, this opulent spa room (created by Poolman of Wisconsin in Eau Claire) indulges the senses while creating the ultimate home spa atmosphere.

Depending on the climate where you live, you might want to consider a radiant heating system beneath the floor of your spa room to take the chill out of stone and tile surfaces during winter months.

Lighting. Electricity and water are a dangerous combination, so plan the lighting around your indoor spa carefully. Don't install light fixtures directly over your spa, because the bulbs may be difficult to access when it's time to change them. Instead, incorporate as much natural lighting as possible by using skylights and floor-to-ceiling windows. Natural light also lets you grow real plants in the room, further enhancing the outdoor feeling.

Use wall sconces and recessed ceiling fixtures around the room's perimeter to set the mood. Prefabricated spas come with at least one underwater light, which in many cases can be adjusted for brightness. And some come with colored lenses or colored bulbs that let you change the water's hue from a sunset red to a Mediterranean blue.

Beyond the Spa

A growing trend is for the spa environment, whether indoors or outdoors, to be part of a larger entertainment and relaxation area. When designing your spa oasis, don't overlook the possibility of installing adjacent facilities, such as a changing room, a shower, a steam room, a sauna, exercise facilities, a wet bar, or an entertainment system that includes audio and video equipment with surround-sound speakers. You'll also want to incorporate comfortable, casual furniture made from practical material, such as vinyl, teak, or aluminum, that won't be harmed when someone sits down wearing a wet swimsuit. Many of today's popular outdoor furniture styles look equally fine indoors.

2 Getting the Most out of Hot Tubs

Hot swirling water. Bubbling jets. Therapeutic hydromassage. What's not to like about spas? For me, nothing erases a bad day, soothes sore muscles, or eliminates stress like 20 minutes in a steamy hot tub.

I realized these benefits long before I purchased my first spa. Years of business travel had afforded me the opportunity to soak in enough hotel spas to suffer chronic wrinkles on my fingers and toes. When the opportunity arose to install a hot tub in my own backyard, I didn't think twice.

◀ A long soak in your steamy hot tub is the perfect way to relax and rejuvenate after a long and stressful day.

My experience is not entirely unique. Most people have their first hot tub encounter at a hotel or health club. And sooner or later, many are wooed into purchasing their own. Whether it's for hydrotherapy, aquatic exercise, stress relief, or marital bliss, the purchase of a hot tub signals better times ahead.

SPA ENJOYMENT AND SAFETY

Imagine yourself reclining in neck-deep water, powerful massage jets washing away the worries of the day. For the nearly 400,000 people who buy a new hot tub each year, that's the major benefit of spa ownership. However, there are other advantages to owning a hot tub. Medical research continues to identify new ways to reap the rewards of hot-water therapy, and manufacturers constantly introduce accessories that build on the hot tub experience.

Aquatic Exercise

Though relaxation is the number-one reason to own a hot tub, more and more people are purchasing a hot tub for aquatic exercise. The buoyancy of the water reduces strain on the heart and muscles, making it easier to perform exercises. In fact, your heart works 10 to 20 percent more efficiently when you are immersed in hot water, according to the National Spa and Pool Institute. That's partially because your body weighs about 90 percent less when it is submerged in water up to the neck, so movement is easier.

In addition to relaxing muscles, hot water can decrease muscle pain and stiffness. Some spas have exercise and fitness equipment incorporated into their design. Others are large enough to be called swim spas, which include a jet on one end that creates a current for bathers to swim against. (See page 16

▲ Soaking in a hot tub for a few minutes before and after an aquatic exercise regimen is a great way to loosen and relax muscles.

for more information on swim spas and fitness spas.)

When exercising in warm water, keep in mind that extremely hot water may not be safe and is not necessary to get results. Moderate heat — about 90°F (32°C) — is just as effective and easier for the body to tolerate.

When first entering a spa, relax and enjoy the water before beginning your exercises. When your muscles and joints feel comfortable and relaxed, slowly begin your exercise routine. Soak in the water for a few minutes after exercising to allow your muscles to relax again before getting out of the water.

Health Benefits

Medical research has found that hot-water therapy can help with a number of health issues. However, it's important to consult a physician prior to beginning any new health regimen. Your doctor can help you develop a hot tub treatment that's individualized for your specific needs. That said, here are some health areas addressed by hot tub use.

Arthritis. Hot-water therapy is known to relieve arthritis pain for many patients who suffer from this debilitating disease. In fact, the Arthritis Foundation (www.arthritis.org) is a staunch advocate of hot-water therapy. There are many effective ways to minimize pain and loss of motion from arthritis, so you should work with your doctor and other health professionals to develop a custom program of treatment that takes into account the type of arthritis you have, how it affects you, the severity of the disease, and the joints affected.

Diabetes. More than 15 million Americans have diabetes, according to the American Diabetes Association. And the only way to manage the problems and side effects that accompany the disease is to closely monitor blood glucose (sugar) levels. A study published in the September 6, 1999, issue of the *New England Journal of Medicine* found that hot tub therapy might help those suffering from type 2 diabetes by reducing their blood sugar levels and improving sleep patterns. According to the study, the effects of hot-water therapy can mimic some of the effects of physical exercise, which is recommended for patients with type 2 diabetes mellitus. In the independent study, led by Dr. Philip L. Hooper at the McKee Medical Center in Loveland, Colorado, patients with type 2 diabetes were required to soak in a hot tub for 30 minutes a day, 6 days a week, for 3 weeks. The results: Average blood sugar levels were reduced by an average of 13 percent. One of the subjects was even able to reduce his daily dose of insulin by 18 percent after only 10 days of therapy. Though these findings are encouraging for diabetics who have difficulty exercising, it is imperative that anyone with diabetes consult his or her physician before beginning hot tub treatments.

Stress. Like therapeutic massages, spas have the power to release tension, relax muscles, and temporarily reduce stress.

Sleep. According to the Better Sleep Council (www.bettersleep.org), in 2004, 65 percent of Americans were losing sleep due to stress, and 16 percent of Americans experienced stress-induced insomnia. The National Sleep Foundation (www.sleepfoundation.org) recommends a 15-minute hot bath to help relieve stress before sleeping. The foundation points to studies that suggest that soaking in hot water (such as in a hot tub or bath) before retiring to bed can ease the transition into deeper sleep. However, you should exit the spa about 20 to 30 minutes before going to bed to ensure that you are no longer sweating or overheated when you "hit the hay."

High Blood Pressure. The heat causes blood vessels to dilate, which lowers blood pressure. However, never use hot tub therapy to treat any illness or disease without first getting approval from a physician. Be careful not to overdo it. If you begin to feel nauseated or dizzy, slowly get out of the tub and rest.

Accessorize It

Your spa offers years of enjoyment, but the fun and excitement grow exponentially when you begin to add accessories into the mix.

Like frosting on a cake, accessories take something that's perfectly fine the way it is and kick it up a notch, enabling you to experience the item in new and innovative ways.

Think about your car for a moment. Sure, you could have settled for a stripped-down model that would have transported you and your family from the supermarket to soccer practice just fine. But notice how much more enjoyable the ride is and how many more things you can do with your car when you begin to add accessories — everything from CD and DVD players to hands-free telephones to roof racks that carry your bikes, skis, and canoe. Well, the same thing goes for your spa. You'll encounter an endless stream of delightful possibilities when you begin adding accessories to your hot-water oasis.

Like so many accessories that impact our lives, we often don't know how much we "need" them until they are brought to our attention. Over time, the most popular accessories become standard equipment and are no longer viewed as an "add-on" purchase. We saw this happen in the automobile industry with automatic windows, air-conditioning, and airbags. In the spa industry, many accessories are becoming "indispensable," too; many more appeal to individual whims and fancies.

Cover Removal Devices. Covering your spa when it's not in use is smart for several reasons. A cover safeguards the water when adults aren't present to supervise, it reduces evaporation, it lowers heating costs, it helps keep the water clean, and it reduces the rate at which sanitizers dissipate in the water. Any one of these reasons should convince you of the need to cover your spa. However, a spa cover is heavy and can be unwieldy to move. In such cases, some people simply fold open half of their spa cover and enjoy only the

▲ Top: A pop-up television screen enables you to watch a movie or cheer for your favorite team without having to leave the tub. And a remote control allows couch potatoes to be hot-tub potatoes, too. Middle: Retractable, waterproof speakers are a great way to surround yourself with relaxing music. Bottom: A sheer waterfall adds drama and relaxing sounds to the hot tub experience.

HATS OFF

Removal devices for hot tub covers come in a variety of designs to accomodate different types of spa installations. They all, however, simplify the task of removing and replacing the cover.

A simple support bar stores the cover in a flat position.

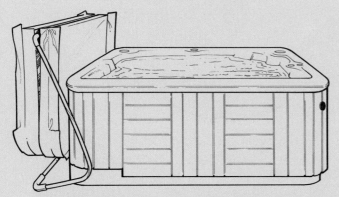

The cover folds over a support bar and hangs at the side.

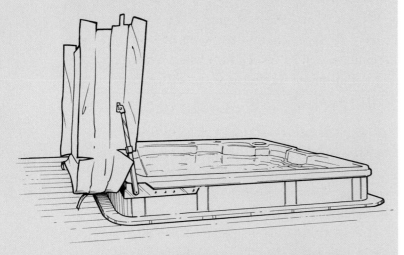

Gas springs assist with lifting and lowering the cover.

exposed portion of the spa, rather than struggling to remove the entire cover. Fortunately, a host of spa cover removal devices on the market make the job of removing and replacing a spa cover as easy as opening and closing the trunk of your car. A cover removal device also helps you properly store the cover so that it doesn't rest on the ground, where it can become distorted or punctured.

Basically, all cover removal systems simplify the handling of the cover. Beyond that, they break down into three general types:

● *Low-end units composed of wood or metal support arms at the lip of the spa.* The arms may or may not be retractable. You fold the spa cover and push it onto these support arms. They hold the cover in a flat position. To replace the cover, you simply push it back over the spa. These units require the most clearance — the width of a folded cover — of all spa cover removal devices and offer no mechanical assistance, except that the cover doesn't need to be lifted off the ground to be replaced.

● *Units made of steel or aluminum that mount to the spa cabinet's rear or sides.* The cover is folded over a support bar, from which the cover hangs as it is pulled or pushed behind the spa. These units typically offer gas spring assistance and require up to 2 feet (0.6 m) of clearance.

● *Units made of steel or aluminum that mount to the top of a spa cabinet or deck.* The cover is folded over a support bar, from which the cover hangs as it is lifted to an upright position, creating a wall or privacy screen. These units typically offer locking gas spring assistance, so they won't blow over in the wind, and require practically no clearance, making them ideal for use in gazebos, up against walls, or in other tight locations.

▲ Colored LED underwater lights allow you to change hues to match your mood, from peaceful blue to sensual red.

Within each type are further differences worth noting. For example, some systems attach directly to the cover, thereby reducing wear and tear on the cover's vinyl hinge. Aesthetically speaking, some units are more visually appealing than others. Some basic wood units tie in nicely with spa skirts, and powder coating on several metal units gives them a finished look.

In the end, a cover removal device will make life easier for you and encourage you to use your spa more often. And anything that entices you to use your hot tub more often is worth consideration.

Spa Fragrances. When it comes to spas, you don't need much more than the therapeutic pounding of jets to put a smile on your face. Nevertheless, there are ways to expand the spa experience. One of the most popular ways to do this is with spa fragrances. These concentrated formulas use the science of aromatherapy to create fragrances that aid in stress relief and awaken the senses. You can choose from citrus blends, floral scents, and herbal extracts. Fragrances come in liquid or granular form, and you simply pour as much as you want into the water to achieve the desired strength. Fragrances dissipate after 15 minutes or so, at which time you can add more of the same fragrance or switch scents to suit your mood.

Lights. Most spas are equipped with an underwater light, but you can quickly change the mood by installing a color-changing light that turns the water to a seductive red or a tranquil blue. Some underwater lights use clusters of different-colored low-voltage LED bulbs. Others spa manufacturers may supply colored lenses that fit over the underwater light's clear lens.

▶ By recessing a spa into a wooden deck, you can create the appearance of an in-ground hot tub.

Music and Movies. Some portable spas now incorporate CD and DVD players with built-in waterproof speakers and monitors. Combined with a floating remote control, your favorite tunes or flicks are just a push button away.

Iceboxes. Some high-end spas boast integrated refrigerators that keep refreshments cold and convenient. Others have ice buckets built right into the spa shell.

Simple Pleasures. Often the smallest accessories are the ones that bring us the most enjoyment, such as waterproof playing cards, plush bathrobes, floating drink holders, and even rubber duckies.

Safety Tips

The benefits of hot tub use far outweigh the risks. Nevertheless, you should be aware of the potential dangers associated with hot tubs. Poor sanitation and improper use are the major risk factors contributing to spa-related illness and injury. Following are some tips for ensuring that you and your loved ones have only happy memories of your spa moments.

Some Concerns. If you have any medical conditions that could be exacerbated by hot tub use, consult your doctor before purchasing a spa. Conditions that could raise a red flag are lung or heart disease, circulatory problems, high or low blood pressure, diabetes, multiple sclerosis, skin irritations, and any other serious illnesses.

Heat Exhaustion. New hot tub users should vary the temperature and length of their stay until they can determine what is most comfortable. Start with a few minutes and slowly extend the time in the water, depending on how you feel. For most people, soaking for 10 to 15 minutes in water temperatures of 98 to 104°F (37 to 40°C) is enjoyable. Never heat your spa over 104°F (40°C). Children and elderly people are more prone to becoming overheated and may need to soak for less time.

If you begin to feel nauseated, light-headed, or dizzy, slowly exit the tub and rest for a while. Exiting too quickly could cause you to fall or faint. As a precaution, you may want to use a spa thermometer to double-check the temperature reading on your control panel before getting into the water.

A spa thermometer costs about $5 and can be tethered to a handrail so it dangles in the water and registers current temperature.

Entrance and Exit. Climbing in and out of a spa can be a precarious proposition for even the most agile. If necessary, make sure grab rails are available. Also, place steps next to aboveground spa installations to make it easier to enter and exit. At night, make sure the underwater light is on so that the spa surface is visible to bathers entering the water.

Overuse. Sometimes too much of a good thing can cause more problems. If joint swelling, stiffness, or pain increases, discontinue spa use and consult your doctor.

Alcohol. A lot of people like to sip on a beer or a glass of wine while in the hot tub. But mixing alcohol and spa use is never a good idea. Alcohol may cause sleepiness, drowsiness, or changes in blood pressure that could lead to drowning. The same goes for recreational drug use.

Pregnancy. Pregnant women should not enter a hot tub without first consulting their doctor. Typically, hot tub use is not recommended for pregnant women because the heat could cause damage to the fetus.

Hygiene. Always shower before entering the spa to reduce the amount of contaminants introduced into the water, including sweat, makeup, body lotions, and deodorants. Don't allow people with infections or open wounds to use the spa. Also, don't allow people — especially kids in diapers — to bathe if they have diarrhea. Fecal matter can contaminate the water and infect others with any number of waterborne germs. Bathers should wash their hands with soap and water after using the toilet or changing diapers so that germs don't make their way to the spa.

Supervision. Never allow children to use the spa without adult supervision, even if you think they are accomplished swimmers.

Fencing. Many municipalities require fencing around outdoor spas. To be considered a safety fence, the barrier must be at least 48 inches (122 cm) high and not have any openings a child might squeeze through. It should also be extremely difficult to get a hand- or toehold on the fence for climbing. Although any fence can be climbed by a resourceful child given enough time, the fence should be designed in such a way that it's at least difficult to surmount. Popular styles of spa fencing include chain link, ornamental wrought iron or aluminum, and wooden picket. Fences that allow outsiders to see into your spa area are less of a deterrent than those that block the view entirely. Also, fences that are surrounded by thorny shrubs and flowerbeds are less likely to be climbed than those that offer a clear runway.

Gates and Doors. Self-latching gates and self-closing doors protect against unauthorized and unsupervised entry into the spa area. It's important to note that the latch must be set above the reach of toddlers and small children to ensure its effectiveness. A variety of self-closing devices can accommodate different door styles, including hinged and sliding.

Door Alarms. If installed and used according to the manufacturer's instructions, these devices sound an alarm when someone tries to enter the pool area. Door alarms typically have a pass/reset button or keypad that turns off the alarm temporarily while an adult or authorized user passes through the door. Keep the button or keypad out of the reach of children, and resist the temptation to deactivate the alarm when doorway traffic is heavy.

Locking Covers. Whenever the spa is not in use, make sure that the spa cover is latched and locked to prevent unsupervised or unauthorized access to the tub. Most spa covers are equipped with straps that easily snap into latches attached to the sides of the spa.

Sanitation. Maintain proper sanitizer levels at all times. During periods of heavy spa use, you may need to ask bathers to exit the tub so you can test the water. If you need to add a sanitizer, allow the chemicals to circulate for at least 15 minutes before retesting. Once the sanitizer level is back to an acceptable range, invite bathers back into the water. (For specifics on water chemistry, see Spa Maintenance below.)

Ventilation. For indoor spa installations, you need to ensure that you have adequate ventilation to avoid moisture damage to property, as well as illnesses such as hypersensitivity pneumonitis, which can be caused by the breathing of contaminated aerosolized water particles. See page 25 for information about designing an indoor spa installation, and see Hot Tub Lung on page 52 for information about hypersensitivity pneumonitis.

Entrapment. Most new spas are designed with multiple inlets so that if one is blocked by a body part, the other one can handle the intake flow without creating enough suction at the other inlet to entrap the bather. Nevertheless, don't use a spa that has a missing or broken grate over a drain. All swimmers, especially children, should be told not to play with these devices. And people with long hair should not submerge their heads near this inlet, where the suction can cause their hair to become tangled in the fitting, resulting in entrapment.

Electrical Devices. Common sense tells us that we shouldn't use electrical devices such as portable radios and CD players where they could fall into the water and electrocute bathers. Whenever possible, use battery-operated appliances instead. Make sure all outside electrical outlets are equipped with a GFCI (ground fault circuit interrupter) to protect against electrical shock.

Telephones. Install a phone or keep a cordless telephone near the spa for use in an emergency. Along with the phone, have a list of emergency contact names and numbers. It's also a good idea to have your own address on the list in case a guest or someone unfamiliar with your address is making the call.

Glassware. Don't use glassware around spas. Broken glass poses a serious danger to barefoot bathers and is nearly impossible to remove from the water. Instead, use plastic or paper cups and dishes.

Storms. Don't soak in your outdoor hot tub during lightning or rainstorms because of the threat of electrocution if lighting were to strike the water.

SPA MAINTENANCE

As a spa owner, your primary goal is to soak in your hot tub as often as possible. Your primary responsibility, however, is to ensure that the water is properly balanced and sanitized so that spa users don't get sick. To do this, you need some basic knowledge of water chemistry and a familiarity with the various types of sanitizers available for use in pools and spas. If you're diligent about testing the water and adding the proper amounts of the required chemicals, you'll be rewarded with clean, healthy water. If not,

CALCULATING THE VOLUME OF YOUR SPA

The amount of chemicals you add to your spa is dependent on how much water you are treating. Here's how to calculate the approximate number of gallons in two typical spa shapes. To convert gallons to liters, simply multiply the number of gallons by 3.7854.

Circular Spa

For a circular spa, first determine the radius, which is half the diameter, in feet. Then square the radius (i.e., multiply it by itself). Then multiply this number by 3.14 (the value of pi), and then again by the average depth in feet. Finally, multiply by 7.5 (the number of gallons in a cubic foot).

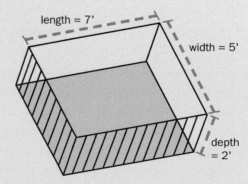

Example: Diameter = 7', so radius = 3.5'

$$3.5 \times 3.5 = 12.25$$
$$12.25 \times 3.14 = 38.465$$
$$38.465 \times 2 = 76.93$$
$$76.93 \times 7.5 = 576.975 \text{ gallons}$$
$$(2,184 \text{ L})$$

Square or Rectangular Spa

Multiply the length by the width, then multiply by the average depth, in feet. Finally, multiply by 7.5.

Example:
$$5 \times 7 = 35$$
$$35 \times 2 = 70$$
$$70 \times 7.5 = 525 \text{ gallons}$$
$$(1,987 \text{ L})$$

▲ Spa water doesn't take care of itself. Yet with regular testing and routine chemical treatments, you can minimize the time you spend correcting water problems and maximize the time you spend enjoying your aquatic paradise.

you could encounter a host of problems, including algae growth, staining, and corrosive water that irritates the eyes and skin.

In some areas of the country, you can hire a service company to manage the routine care of your spa. However, do-it-yourself maintenance will not only save you money but also provide you with the peace of mind that comes with knowing exactly how clean and safe your water is at all times.

For those who like to know the why behind the how of hot-water chemistry, this section is for you. Keep in mind that there is no standard water treatment method for every spa. Rather, there are guidelines, parameters, and

recommendations. Ultimately, it's up to you to determine which method of water treatment you prefer.

A Balancing Act

Keeping your spa water sanitized is your primary goal. For any sanitizer to work well, however, the water needs to be balanced. Five factors contribute to water balance: pH, total alkalinity, calcium hardness, total dissolved solids (TDS), and temperature. With the exception of temperature, each factor can be measured with a test kit available from a pool and spa supply dealer, as well as some home improvement stores and mass merchants. If the values are on the low side, the results can be metal corrosion, surface etching, and staining. If they are on the high side, you may see cloudy water, staining, and mineral deposits. In either case, soakers are likely to experience eye and skin irritation.

Because a change in one factor can affect the others, your challenge is to "balance" the water using various types of chemicals, also available from most hot tub dealers. The process isn't as hard as you may think, as long as you understand how each factor contributes to the overall balance.

First, it's important to note the volume of your spa, because the amount of chemicals you'll add depends a lot on how many gallons or liters of water you are treating. The volume of water in a spa is usually noted in the manufacturer's owner's manual, but if you own a custom spa, you may need to calculate its volume on your own using basic geometry. Refer to Calculating the Volume of Your Spa, page 39, for easy-to-follow formulas.

Now let's look at the five water balance factors and how they affect the quality of your spa water. Most of them are easily monitored using test strips.

COMFORT ZONE

The pH scale ranges from 0 to 14, with 7 being neutral. Numbers below 7 indicate an acidic state, and numbers above 7 indicate an alkaline state. The ideal range for spa water is 7.4 to 7.6.

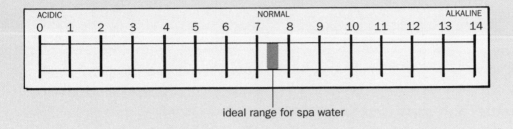

ideal range for spa water

pH

Water pH is a measure of acidity or alkalinity. The pH scale runs from 0 to 14, with 7 being neutral. Lower values are acidic, and higher values are alkaline. The acceptable range for spa water is 7.2 to 7.8, though many experts recommend an even narrower range of 7.4 to 7.6. Not coincidentally, this is the same pH range as that of human eyes — one reason why a proper pH level is important for bather comfort.

When pH is low, the water is acidic. Acidic water can etch metals and plaster, stain plaster finishes, and cause bather discomfort, such as skin and eye irritation. Low pH also causes sanitizers to dissipate quickly.

When the pH is high, the water is alkaline, or scale producing. Alkaline water can be cloudy and form scale deposits on the spa surface and equipment. With high pH levels, sanitizers becomes less effective, and skin and eye irritation may occur.

Testing pH. The easiest way to monitor pH is with test strips, although more accurate results can be achieved with liquid test kits. With test strips, you simply dip or swirl the strip in the water according to the manufac-turer's instructions, wait the prescribed amount of time, and match the color results on the strip with a colorimeter printed on the canister. Liquid test kits involve taking a water sample, adding a specified amount of reagent, and then comparing the results to a colorimeter. Both types of testing products are available at pool and spa supply stores. For more tips on testing, see 10 Tips for Accurate Water Testing, page 42.

Adjusting pH. Adding an alkali, such as soda ash (sodium carbonate), to the water will cause the pH value to rise. Adding an acid, such as muriatic acid or sodium bisulfate, to the water will cause the pH value to fall. The pH can also be adjusted through the use of specially designed products, typically sold with names like pH Up or pH Down, that are available from swimming pool and spa supply retailers. Add these products, or your selected alkali or acid, following the instructions on the product label. When adjusting pH, keep in mind that most chemicals used in spas — even those not designed to adjust pH levels, such as sanitizers and aromatherapy fragrances — are acidic or alkaline and therefore will affect the pH level.

10 TIPS FOR ACCURATE WATER TESTING

Balancing spa water becomes a futile task if you don't know how to test the water properly. Everything from improper storage of test kits to incorrect timing can cause false readings — and false readings can prompt you to take the wrong course of action.

First, you need to decide which type of testing method you will use. The most accurate results tend to come from liquid test kits. These kits require you to add drops of chemical reagents to a sample of water from your spa and match the color it yields with those on a chart. An easier method is test strips, which typically require you to dip or swirl a strip in the water sample and match the resulting colors on the strip to the corresponding charts on the test strip bottle.

Test strips are available for measuring chlorine levels, bromine levels, pH, and alkalinity. Liquid test kits are available for measuring those plus calcium hardness.

Most pool and spa dealers offer free professional water testing; all you have to do is bring in a water sample in a clean container. Many dealers will even print out an analysis that tells you precisely which chemicals, and how much of each, to add to your spa.

That said, you will still need to test your water regularly. To ensure the most accurate results for your analysis, follow these guidelines.

1 TAKE YOUR WATER SAMPLE from at least 12 to 18 inches (30 to 45 cm) below the surface. Water near the surface often has a lower sanitizer residual than the rest of the water and can have a higher pH due to evaporation and UV rays near the surface. To get a good sample, invert a clean jar or vial and plunge it up to your elbow beneath the surface of the water. Then upright the jar or vial and fill it.

2 DON'T TAKE WATER SAMPLES FROM NEAR RETURN INLETS. If the spa has an in-line chemical feeder, the concentration of sanitizer will be higher there than in the rest of the pool or spa.

3 TEST SAMPLES FROM SEVERAL LOCATIONS if your spa has dead spots — areas with poor circulation.

4 **ALWAYS USE A CAP,** not your fingers, to seal a test jar or vial. Otherwise, contaminants from your skin can skew pH readings.

5 **PERFORM TESTS QUICKLY,** before the sample has time to change temperature. Temperature plays a big role in water balance, and you want to test the sample while it's still the same temperature as the rest of the water in your spa.

6 **TO GET AN ACCURATE READ ON COLOR-BASED TESTS,** don't wear sunglasses, and perform the test in natural daylight. Some experts recommend having the sun behind you, holding the test vial at eye level, and holding a piece of white paper at a 45-degree angle behind the test vial to reflect light through it so that you can see the color clearly.

7 **WHEN SQUEEZING DROPS OF LIQUID REAGENTS FROM A BOTTLE,** hold the bottle in a vertical position so that the drops are uniform in size.

8 **MAKE SURE REAGENTS AND TEST STRIPS ARE FRESH.** Some experts recommend replacing reagents and test strips annually. To keep supplies fresh, close bottles of reagents and boxes of test strips as soon as you're finished with them. Make sure your fingers are dry before reaching into a bottle of test strips. And store supplies in a cool, dry place out of sunlight.

9 **DON'T TRY TO SUBSTITUTE REAGENTS** from one test kit with another. The color standards, sample sizes, and reagent concentration may differ between one kit and another.

10 **FOLLOW THE INSTRUCTIONS** on product labels carefully. If a test calls for the sample to be swirled, don't shake it. Shaking could expose the water to oxygen or carbon dioxide, which could skew results. Also, watch the clock. Some test strips are designed to be read immediately, while others call for a waiting period. Waiting too long or reading too soon will not yield an accurate water analysis.

Note: Working with certain acid products can be particularly hazardous. For safety guidelines, see Chemical Safety, page 49.

TOTAL ALKALINITY

Total alkalinity is the sum of all the alkaline substances in the water. The acceptable range for total alkalinity depends on the sanitizer you use. For example, the ideal range for total alkalinity when using bromine (the most popular spa sanitizer) is 100 to 120 parts per million (ppm).

Maintaining proper total alkalinity levels is important because it helps to lock in (or stabilize) pH. In other words, once you have total alkalinity under control, pH will tend to remain constant. In contrast, if alkalinity levels are too low, you're likely to see wide fluctuations in pH.

Testing Total Alkalinity. The same test strips or kits you use to test pH will often measure total alkalinity, too. Be sure, however, to follow the testing guidelines on the packaging, as procedures often differ from one brand of test strips or test kits to another.

Adjusting Total Alkalinity. To raise total alkalinity without raising pH significantly, add sodium bicarbonate (often referred to as baking soda) to the water. If you also want to raise pH, you can use sodium carbonate (often referred to as soda ash), which is a more alkaline chemical compound. If your source water is extremely hard (meaning it contains high levels of calcium and magnesium), it's possible that your total alkalinity levels may be too high. Hard water is not necessarily a problem if pH can be brought into the acceptable range and the water remains clear. Use a pH decreaser or liquid muriatic acid to reduce total alkalinity. Be sure to follow the manufacturer's instructions when applying any spa chemical.

CALCIUM HARDNESS

Calcium hardness is a measure of the water's calcium content and, therefore, relates to the water's corrosive tendencies. Too much calcium in the water causes it to precipitate out of the water and leads to deposits on surfaces and piping. Too little calcium leads to corrosion and etching.

WHEN TO DRAIN

Because of heavy bather loads and the constant addition of chemicals, spa water can take on a high concentration of dissolved solids, making the water difficult to balance. To ensure water quality and keep the water easy to balance, drain the spa water at least every three months — more often if the spa is used heavily.

To better determine how often you should change the water, use this formula:

spa size in gallons ÷ (number of daily bathers x 3) = number of days between water changes

Example:

If you have a 500-gallon spa that's used by two people every day:

500 ÷ (2 x 3) = 500 ÷ 6 = 83

You should change the water every 83 days, or every 2 to 3 months.

Between drainings, you can reduce the contaminants (body oil, dirt, lotions, deodorants, makeup, hair products, etc.) in your spa water by having bathers shower before entering the tub.

The ideal range for calcium hardness for spas is 150 to 250 ppm, though some manufacturers may recommend a narrower range, depending on the type of spa shell you have.

Testing Calcium Hardness. You'll need a liquid test kit to monitor the level.

Adjusting Calcium Hardness. Low calcium hardness tends to be a more common problem than high calcium hardness. To raise the level, carefully add predissolved calcium chloride. In the rare instance that the level is too high, replace some of the pool or spa water with fresh water.

TOTAL DISSOLVED SOLIDS

The term *total dissolved solids* (TDS) refers to the concentration of conductive chemicals, bather waste, and other solids that can accumulate in the water, particularly when the water evaporates. You cannot see these solids because they are dissolved in the water, but this does not stop them from corroding metal parts. High TDS also reduces sanitizer efficiency and can make water taste salty. TDS should never be allowed to exceed 1,500 ppm over the start-up level, which is the amount of total dissolved solids measured when the spa is initially filled with fresh water.

TDS is a major concern for spas because of the high water temperatures, which lead to fast evaporation and quick concentration of dissolved solids. Plus, the bather load is heavy in a spa compared to that of a pool, meaning that higher concentrations of solids are introduced to the water via sweat, body oil, soap, shampoo, sunscreen, and even urine.

Testing Total Dissolved Solids. TDS can be tested only with a liquid test kit designed for professional use. If high TDS is a concern, you should take a water sample to a pool and spa supply store for professional testing.

Adjusting Total Dissolved Solids. The easiest way to lower TDS in a spa is to replace some or all of the water with fresh water. Even if the source water is hard and contains lots of dissolved solids, it will still contain fewer dissolved solids than the used water in your spa.

TEMPERATURE

Temperature plays an important role in water balance because calcium becomes less soluble as water temperature increases and more soluble as the temperature decreases. In other words, warm water tends to be more basic and scale producing, while colder water is more corrosive. In a spa, where the water temperature is consistently over 100°F (38°C), calcium easily becomes less soluble and needs to be kept in check by closely monitoring the other water balance factors.

Most spas have a built-in thermostat that transmits the temperature to the spa's control panel. As a backup, it's a good idea to use a separate spa thermometer tethered to a handrail and dangled in the water. These thermometers cost about $5 and are available from spa supply outlets.

BRINGING THEM TOGETHER

So there you have them: the five fickle factors that contribute to balanced spa water. As you may be thinking, maintaining perfect water balance can be tricky at times. However, the main factor you'll be concerned with is pH, which is easy to monitor and adjust.

For those who take their water chemistry seriously, a mathematical formula can help you better understand the intricate relationship among all of these factors. Called the saturation index, it was derived from the work of Wilfred F. Langelier, who was commissioned in the 1930s to discover a method for laying down a thin layer of scale on the water-distribution piping of a large city to protect

RECOMMENDED WATER BALANCE FOR RESIDENTIAL SPAS

COMPONENT	MINIMUM LEVEL	IDEAL LEVEL	MAXIMUM LEVEL
Free chlorine (ppm)	2.0	3.0–5.0	10.0
Combined chlorine (ppm)	0.0	0.0	0.2
Bromine (ppm)	2.0	4.0–6.0	10.0
PHMB — biguanide (ppm)	30.0	30.0–50.0	50.0
pH	7.2	7.4–7.6	7.8
Total alkalinity (ppm as $CaCO_3$)	60	80–100*/ 100–120**	180
Calcium hardness (ppm as $CaCO_3$)	100	150–250	800
Total dissolved solids	—	—	1,500 ppm over start-up TDS level
Temperature	personal preference	personal preference	104°F (40°C)
Ozone (ppm)	—	—	0.1***

* For calcium hypochlorite, lithium hypochlorite, or sodium hypochlorite
** For sodium dichlor, trichlor, chlorine gas, or bromine
*** Over 8-hour time, weighted average

Source: Reprinted from National Spa and Pool Institute, *Standard for Residential Swimming Pools*, ANSI/NSPI-5 2003

the cast-iron pipes from corrosion. Applied to spa water, the index looks like this:

$$SI = pH + TF + CH + ALK - CONSTANT$$

SI = saturation index

pH = measured pH

TF = temperature factor

CH = measured calcium hardness

ALK = measured alkalinity minus cyanurate alkalinity, which is the alkalinity attributed to cyanurate acid, sometimes used to stabilize pH

CONSTANT = combined factor that corrects for temperature, as well as the strength and concentration of ions in the water

Water is considered balanced when the SI equals zero. An SI of +/−0.3 is considered acceptable. Above 0.3 indicates that conditions are ripe for cloudiness and scaling; below −0.3 warns of possible corrosive conditions.

This type of advanced mathematics could drive the typical spa owner to rethink his or her purchase. Fortunately, at least one company has produced a simple-to-use tool that does the math for you. Developed by Taylor Technologies, the Watergram is simply two circular charts, one small and one large, laid together and riveted through the center. The small inner circle is printed with numbers for pH and calcium hardness, while the outer circle has numbers for total alkalinity and temperature. Let's say you've measured the pH and taken the temperature of your spa water. You'd locate that pH reading on the inner wheel and the temperature reading on the outer wheel. When you turn the inner wheel so that the pH reading and the tem-

perature reading are aligned, the wheel shows you whether total alkalinity or calcium hardness needs to be adjusted.

As mentioned previously, test strips are a convenient and simple way to get an adequate reading on pH and total alkalinity. Plus, most test strips also have pads to test the level of chlorine or bromine sanitizer in the water, making them a quick and efficient way to stay on top of your water quality.

Sanitizers and Oxidizers

Now that you understand what it means to balance spa water, let's look at the chemicals that disinfect the water, making it clean enough to soak in. Close monitoring and adjustments of sanitizer levels are crucial to a healthy spa experience. High water temperatures create an ideal breeding ground for algae and bacteria. Plus, a heavy bather load makes it difficult to maintain the proper amount of sanitizer in the water at all times. Compared to a swimming pool, the low volume of spa water in relation to the number of bathers makes hot tub water a bit more difficult to manage. For example, it's estimated that 2 people in a hot tub create contamination proportionate to that of 60 people in a typical swimming pool. If that doesn't illustrate the importance of spa water care, consider this: One person in a spa produces about 1 liter of sweat per hour.

Despite the grossness of such alarming facts, rest assured that hot tub use is safe and healthy if water is sanitized and balanced per industry standards (see Recommended Water Balance for Residential Spas, at left).

The two categories of disinfectants are sanitizers and oxidizers. Sanitizers kill pollutants like algae and bacteria. Oxidizers (often sold in concentrated forms called shock) will "burn up" or remove any accumulated waste products such as sweat, body oil, shampoo, soap, and urine. Spa water needs both a sanitizer for day-to-day use and an oxidizer for periodic shocking. Some common sanitizers, such as chlorine and bromine, also oxidize. Others, such as biguanide, are only sanitizers and require a separate oxidizing chemical to work effectively.

CHLORINE

Chlorine is both a sanitizer and an oxidizer. Its low cost relative to other sanitizing chemicals makes it a popular choice for swimming pools; however, it isn't very stable at high temperatures, which is why in spas it's more often used as a shock than a routine sanitizer.

Chlorine also dissipates quickly in sunlight. On a sunny day, as much as 95 percent of active chlorine can be lost in just two hours. That's why chlorine is often paired with a stabilizing agent such as cyanuric acid. There are several types of chlorine, and some — such as dichlor and trichlor — are more stable than others.

It's important to note that some types of chlorine affect pH more than others, so you'll want to take that into account when balancing your spa water and choosing a chlorine sanitizer. A high pH drastically reduces the effectiveness of chlorine because it accelerates the rate at which chlorine molecules break down. Spas that operate at high pH levels require higher levels of chlorine to kill algae and bacteria.

After chlorine is no longer able to kill organisms, it combines with contaminants in the spa to form chloramines, nasty little molecules that can irritate eyes and skin and cause a strong chlorinelike odor. Although many people assume that a strong chlorine odor is an indication that there is too much chlorine in the water, actually the opposite is true. The strong odor usually means that the chlorine in the water is no longer an effective sanitizer and chloramines have formed. The solution to this problem is to superchlorinate or "shock" the water with an oxidizer to eliminate the chloramines.

Testing Chlorine Levels. Easy-to-use test strips and complete test kits are available from spa supply dealers. You'll want to measure "free available" chlorine — the portion of chlorine that's capable of sanitizing, killing germs, and oxidizing organics. When free available chlorine reacts with ammonia waste, it becomes "combined chlorine," also known as chloramines. Whereas free chlorine has no detectable taste or smell at levels up to 10 to 20 ppm, combined chlorine levels as low as 0.2 ppm can create the familiar odor common to heavily used spas (and pools). Combined chlorine has few sanitizing capabilities. For spas, the recommended level for free available chlorine is 3 to 5 ppm.

Adjusting Chlorine Levels. Chlorine comes in many forms: liquid, granular, tablet, stick, and gas. Granules are the most common form used in spas. They are easy to measure and apply, and accidents are less likely to occur because the dry chemical won't splash. To apply granules, carefully sprinkle them as close to the center of the spa as possible, where they have the best chance to circulate and dissolve before coming in contact with the spa's surface. To distribute tablet or stick chlorine, place the tablets or sticks in a floating or in-line dispenser. As water flows through the dispenser, the chlorine is slowly dissolved and released. Some chlorine products contain more free available chlorine than others, so follow the manufacturer's guidelines to determine the correct dose for your size spa.

CHEMICAL SAFETY

Like household cleaners and solvents, spa chemicals can be dangerous. Most can irritate skin, damage eyes, or combust if stored improperly. Follow these guidelines whenever handling spa chemicals.

● *Store sanitizers* in a cool, dry place away from other chemicals, out of direct sunlight, and out of the reach of children and pets.

● *Do not store* liquid chemicals above other chemicals, including garden fertilizers and insecticides, where they could possibly drip and cause a dangerous chemical reaction.

● *Wear safety goggles* and rubber gloves when mixing and dispensing chemicals.

● *If a chemical spill occurs,* follow the cleanup instructions given on the product label.

● *Never mix* different types of products together.

● *Do not smoke* when using products.

● *If mixing with water is required,* never add water to chemicals. Rather, add chemicals to water to eliminate harmful splashing and gassing.

● *Use clean, dry* plastic cups or scoops for measuring specific products. Never put a wet measuring scoop back in a container.

● *Do not inhale* fumes or allow products to contact eyes, ears, nose, or mouth.

● *Always follow* the manufacturer's instructions for any spa or pool chemical.

● *Read the first-aid instructions* given on each product's label before using it. Have emergency medical and poison control center phone numbers handy at all times.

● *Keep products away* from lawns and landscaping.

BROMINE

Chlorine is the most popular sanitizer for pools, but bromine is the sanitizer of choice for stand-alone spas because bromine is more effective at high water temperatures. Though bromine is quickly depleted in sunlight (about 65 percent of active bromine can be depleted in a couple of hours), it works well in spas because they are typically covered when not in use. A major advantage of bromine is that it can be regenerated. That means spent bromine can be reactivated by adding an oxidizing chemical, such as chlorine or potassium monopersulfate.

Testing Bromine Levels. Test methods for bromine levels are similar to those used for chlorine, except there is no way to distinguish between combined bromine and free available bromine. Therefore, you'll be measuring total bromine residual. The ideal range of bromine in residential spas is 4 to 6 ppm.

Adjusting Bromine Levels. Bromine is most often sold as slow-dissolving tablets. The tablets can be placed in a floating or in-line dispenser that allows water to pass through and gradually dissolve the tablets, providing a steady supply of hypobromous acid to the spa water. The fastest way to raise the

HEAVY METAL

Mineral purifiers help keep spa water sanitary. As water flows through a mineral purifier containing silver, copper, and zinc, ions are dispersed into the water, where they kill bacteria. Though this technology doesn't eliminate the need for chemical sanitizers, it can greatly reduce the amount of chemicals you need to add to your spa water.

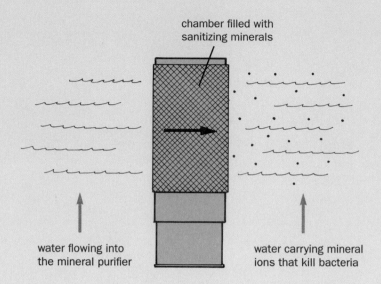

chamber filled with sanitizing minerals

water flowing into the mineral purifier

water carrying mineral ions that kill bacteria

bromine level is to add a bromine shock, such as chlorine or potassium monopersulfate, which will regenerate the bromine bank.

BIGUANIDE

Biguanide was first developed as a presurgery antimicrobial scrub. It is the only nonhalogen sanitizer and oxidizer available for spas. (Both chlorine and bromine belong to the halogen family of chemicals.) Some spa owners prefer biguanide because it is less susceptible to UV rays than chlorine and bromine, it doesn't require a stabilizer, it doesn't degrade with high temperatures or changes in pH, and it usually is applied only every couple of weeks.

With biguanide, the water doesn't smell of chlorine, of course, and it reduces the surface tension of water, which creates a smoother feel. And at recommended concentrations, biguanide won't irritate the skin or eyes.

On the downside, biguanide is more costly than chlorine and bromine; it has a tendency to gum up filters; and it is incompatible with chlorine, bromine, copper-based chemicals

(such as certain algaecides), and nonchlorine shock (such as potassium monopersulfate).

Several companies offer complete biguanide spa care systems, which tell you exactly how to use each product. Follow the instructions carefully and you shouldn't have any problems.

Testing Biguanide Levels. Biguanide levels are monitored with special test kits. To ensure proper use, follow the manufacturer's testing and application guidelines precisely.

Adjusting Biguanide Levels. Biguanide is available in liquid form. The acronym for its chemical name is PHMB, which you may see on the package label. You'll need to add biguanide to spa water only about every 10 to 14 days, but you should still test the water regularly to make sure it is balanced. Follow the manufacturer's directions carefully to determine how much biguanide to add to your spa and how often. And always check with your biguanide dealer before adding supplemental chemicals to biguanide-treated water to make sure they are compatible.

SHOCK

As mentioned above, oxidizing chemicals come in a concentrated form called shock, which is used to supersanitize spa water. In addition to regenerating bromine, shocking burns up bacteria, algae, nitrogen compounds, and smelly ammonia that have not been removed through routine sanitization. Maintaining the proper sanitizer residual will keep your spa safe for bathing, but shocking the water is sometimes necessary to remove dead bacteria and organic matter that could cause skin and eye irritation, cloudy water, and foul odors.

The best time to shock your spa is after sundown, which eliminates the dissipating effect of the sun's ultraviolet rays, or after heavy use. Some shocks, such as chlorine, require bathers to wait until the residual has dropped below 10 ppm before getting in the water. Others, such as monopersulfate, simply regenerate the bromine already in the water, so there is no need to wait before entering the spa. Before adding a spa shock, however, always bring the water balance factors into their proper ranges.

AUTOMATIC SANITIZERS

If you have the money and would prefer the convenience and peace of mind of an automatic sanitizer, here are a few options.

Chlorine and Bromine Generators. These electrical units create chlorine or bromine from special salts added to the water. Some units regenerate a bromine bank already in the water. Chlorine and bromine generators are great for maintaining a sanitizer residual, although periodic shocking is still required.

Ozonators. An ozonator produces and releases ozone, an effective sanitizer, into spa water. However, ozone doesn't last long in a water environment. Once it kills bacteria,

the ozone reverts to oxygen and either dissolves into the water or escapes into the air. There is no easy way to ensure a sufficient ozone residual as new contaminants are introduced. Therefore, an ozonator must be used in conjunction with small amounts of a chemical sanitizer.

There are two types of ozonators: UV and corona discharge. A UV unit creates ozone with a special lightbulb, which needs to be replaced after many months. A corona discharge unit has a special cell that produces ozone. Corona discharge ozonators cost more than UV ozonators, but they don't have any bulbs that need replacing.

Mineral Purifiers. These devices use a combination of silver, copper, and zinc to sanitize water. Some mineral purifiers are simply perforated cylinders that fit inside a spa's cartridge filter, whereas others are plumbed in-line along with the spa's other equipment. As water flows through the device and over the mineral bed, it picks up ions that kill bacteria. Such mineral purifiers last several months before they need replacing. Another type of mineral purifier is an ionizer, which is an electrical device that introduces silver, copper, and zinc ions into the water. Mineral purifiers, however, do not create a sanitizing residual, so they must be used in conjunction with a chemical sanitizer.

Routine Care

When it comes to the routine care of your spa, you'll be happy to know that several chemical manufacturers offer simple, step-by-step maintenance programs that tell you which chemicals to add to your spa water and how and when to do so. If you stay on schedule and test the water regularly, you'll prevent many of the problems that can plague mismanaged spa water.

HOT TUB LUNG

Hypersensitivity pneumonitis, or "hot tub lung," is a rare disease caused by inhaling bacterial fragments called endotoxins, which have become aerosolized by splashing and steaming water. It is much less of a concern in outdoor spas, where adequate ventilation is not an issue. Hypersensitivity pneumonitis causes an allergic and inflammatory reaction, but it is not contagious. Symptoms include lack of appetite, fever, tiredness, night sweats, cough, tightness of chest, and weight loss. Sometimes it is misdiagnosed as tuberculosis or some other lung disease.

Though hypersensitivity pneumonitis is associated with indoor hot tub use, it has also been connected with indoor pools (where it may be referred to as "lifeguard lung"), fountains, and humidifiers. According to the National Spa and Pool Institute, several factors are needed for this disease to occur. First, there needs to be a water circulation system harboring a large number of gram-negative bacteria — the type of bacteria containing endotoxins in cell walls. The bacteria are usually harbored in biofilm, a slime that can grow in pipes and filters. Biofilms can form and become ensconced on a surface during periods of inadequate sanitization. These biofilms can then protect the bacteria from later exposure to sanitizers. Eventually, the biofilm may be disrupted by a violent action, such as the start of hydrotherapy

jets. This disruption can release large numbers of bacteria into the water. The sanitizer breaks down the physical structure of the bacteria and releases endotoxins into the water. Insufficient treatment at this point allows the endotoxins to remain in the water and potentially become aerosolized.

Even if these conditions are met, it's still rare for someone to contract hypersensitivity pneumonitis. The chance of contracting the disease seems to be related to the frequency, duration, and intensity of exposure.

The best way to prevent hypersensitivity pneumonitis is to maintain an effective level of sanitizer in the spa water at all times. Indoor spas require adequate ventilation to ensure a constant supply of fresh air, and proper water balance and effective filtration are also necessary. To reduce the potential for endotoxins, water should be changed on a regular basis (see When to Drain, page 44 for guidelines on how often to change water).

Spas that have not been properly maintained, or that have been out of operation even for a short period of time, should be sanitized before use. After applying a sanitizer, allow the spa water to circulate for about one hour so that the sanitizer is distributed throughout the system. During this time, the jets and aerator should be activated to expose the entire system to the sanitizer.

If you're diligent about caring for your spa water, you may never encounter a problem with quality and sanitization. If you are confronted with a problem — be it cloudy water or algae growth — don't despair. The next section addresses some of the most common spa water problems.

In the meantime, let's walk through the basic steps for draining a spa and starting it up with fresh water:

1. Disconnect the power. Spas are typically hardwired to the home's electrical system, with a ground fault circuit interrupter (GFCI) located near the spa. Disconnect the power at the GFCI to ensure that the spa pumps aren't activated during the cleaning process.

2. Drain the spa. All prefabricated spas are equipped with a drain valve. This is located at the bottom of the spa either behind the cabinet door or along the exterior perimeter. Typically, these valves are equipped with a threaded PVC pipe that can be connected to a garden hose so that the discharged water can be emptied away from the spa area.

3. Clean the filter. While the tub is draining, you should remove the cartridge filter for cleaning. (If you have a custom spa that uses a different type of filtration system, such as sand or diatomaceous earth, refer to the owner's manual for cleaning instructions. If the spa is part of a pool/spa combination, then you should clean the filter when it's necessary for proper pool maintenance.) The cartridge filter should be cleaned every time you change the water. Cleaning a cartridge filter is simply a matter of removing it from the filter bay and hosing it off. Work from the top down, being sure to focus on the deep recesses of the pleats where dirt and debris accumulate. Don't use an extremely high-

CLEAN SWEEP

Cartridge filters are easy to rinse out. To clean a cartridge filter, simply use a garden hose with a nozzle attachment to spray dirt and debris from the cartridge, concentrating on the crevices between the pleats.

pressure nozzle on your hose when cleaning a cartridge filter because the force of the water can weaken the fabric and hinder filtration. When the cartridge is clean, place it back in the filter bay.

If proper water quality is maintained, a cartridge filter should last one to six years, depending on the quality of the filter. Replace cartridges when they are no longer cleanable, when the webbing of the fabric appears shiny and closed, or when the fabric has begun to deteriorate or tear.

If a filter has been exposed to heavy bather loads and high levels of perspiration and body oils, you may need to soak the cartridge in a cleaning solution overnight before hosing it down. You can purchase a filter-cleaning product from a pool and spa supply store, or you can use 1 cup (0.24 L) of trisodium phosphate or dishwasher detergent mixed with 5 gallons (18.9 L) of water. After soaking, rinse the cartridge thoroughly and place it back in the spa.

If the filter is coated with algae or calcium deposits, you may need to acid-wash it. Do not acid-wash a cartridge filter without first removing all oils and subsequent cleaning solution. Otherwise the acid will destroy the filter element. When you are ready to acid-wash, prepare a solution of 1 part muriatic acid and 20 parts water. Soak the cartridge in the solution just until the solution stops bubbling. Then rinse the cartridge thoroughly and immediately place it back in the spa's filter cartridge holder. Muriatic acid is a toxic substance. Be sure to wear rubber gloves when working with it, and use it in a well-ventilated area. The product label will offer other safety and application guidelines.

4. Clean the shell. Clean the shell with appropriate cleaners and a nonabrasive cloth. Special cleaners are available for spa shells, but you can also use regular tub and tile cleaner. Just avoid harsh cleansers that contain abrasives that might scratch the shell. Then rinse the cleanser from the surface and drain it away with the rest of the dirty water from the hot tub.

To maintain your acrylic spa's luster, now is a good time to apply a surface polish or wax used to restore the finish of fiberglass tubs and showers (not the kind designed for automobiles or furniture). Some products are specially formulated for spa surfaces and can be purchased from hot tub supply retailers. Use a soft cotton cloth to buff the surface to a shiny finish.

5. Fill the spa. After you close the drain valve, refill the tub with fresh water, stopping when the water level is at least 1 inch (2.5 cm) above the highest jet. Another good gauge is to fill the spa until it reaches the middle of the skimmer or waterline tile. If you are using a garden hose to fill the spa, you may wish to first let the water run for several minutes to flush out any of the bacteria that sometimes linger in garden hoses. Never use softened water to fill your spa, because its corrosive properties will damage spa equipment.

6. Clean the cover. While the spa is being filled, take this time to clean the spa cover. Most spa covers are made of an insulating foam core that is surrounded by vinyl. Over time, the vinyl can dry out and crack, and it can develop algae stains if the water hasn't been properly sanitized at all times. To extend the life of your spa cover, you should clean it and condition it. Special cleaners and conditioners are available at spa supply stores. Be sure to clean the underside of the cover, too, because this is where bacteria, mold, and algae are most likely to reside. You may need to use a disinfectant (such as Lysol) to remove mold and mildew odors. Some manufacturers have even begun offering specially formulated cover wipes in convenient pop-up dispensers.

After years of service, a spa cover's foam core will absorb water, making a 40-pound (18 kg) cover weigh closer to 100 pounds (45 kg). You can try to dry it out by unzipping the vinyl jacket and removing the foam core for air-drying. If there's a plastic seal around the foam core, don't attempt to unwrap it unless your cover is so waterlogged that your only other option is to buy a new one. Then you're really not risking anything by unwrapping the plastic so that the core can dry out. After the core has dried, attempt to rewrap it in plastic, keeping the seams up away from the water surface and using duct tape to seal all seams before reinserting the core back into the vinyl jacket.

The foam core can begin to warp over time, especially under heavy snow loads. If

▲ A split-level deck hugs this hot tub, with dual risers leading to the top deck. From here, bathers can sit and dangle their feet in the therapeutic water without a full-body submersion.

you notice that rainwater is beginning to collect on the cover, remove the foam core, flip it over, and reinsert it into the vinyl jacket.

7. Turn on the power and adjust controls. Reconnect the GFCI and make sure that the display on the control panel lights up. Turn on the pumps to activate the jets and circulate the water. Also make sure that the air actuator (or blower) is wide open. Then set the heater to the desired temperature, typically 100°F (38°C).

8. Balance and sanitize the water. Balance the water and adjust the sanitizer level. Because water temperature also plays an important role in water balance, you'll need to retest the water when the desired temperature is reached. Make any necessary adjustments. It's best to wait 15 minutes for chemicals to circulate before retesting and making additional adjustments.

If this sounds like more than you can handle, take a deep breath and relax. Most hot tub dealers sell start-up kits that include all of the chemicals you'll need to achieve perfectly balanced water.

9. Install the spa cover. Place the cover squarely on the spa and lock the clasps on the tie-down straps. You shouldn't install the cover immediately after shocking the spa water because the high dose of oxidizer can damage the underside of the cover. Wait until the sanitizer level drops to a safe range (about 10 ppm for bromine) before closing the cover. Also, keeping the cover in place anytime the spa is not in use will reduce the amount of time the heater operates, thereby minimizing operating costs.

10. Enjoy your clean spa. If you maintain a sanitizer residual at all times and shock your spa weekly and after heavy use, you'll eliminate the potential for most water problems. Then all that's left for you to do is enjoy the relaxing, therapeutic benefits of your safe and sanitary spa.

Water Problems

PROBLEM	CAUSE	SOLUTION
Cloudy water	Overload of organic contaminants	Shock the water and bring sanitizer level into the proper range.
	Excessive amounts of hard-to-filter material	Use a clarifier to coagulate small particles so the filter can better remove them.
	Improper levels of pH and/or total alkalinity	Use a pH increaser or decreaser to bring pH into the proper range.
	Dirty filter	Clean the filter.
	High levels of calcium	Use a scale preventive.
Chalky, white scale deposits	High mineral content	Use a scale preventive.
Cloudy, green water	Algae, which was able to grow because of low sanitizer level	Shock the water and bring sanitizer level into the proper range.
Discolored water	Metals are the most common cause of discolored water. Manganese, for example, can give the water a brown, black, or lavender hue. Copper can give the water a greenish tint. Iron can cause a brownish cast.	Use a sequestering agent to keep the metals in solution. Also use a flocculent to cluster the metal particles so they're large enough to filter out.
Unpleasant odor	Chloramines and too many organic contaminants	Shock the water and bring sanitizer level into the proper range.
Eye and skin irritation	Chloramines and too many organic contaminants	Shock the water and bring sanitizer level into the proper range.
	Improper levels of pH and/or total alkalinity	Use a pH increaser or decreaser to bring pH into the proper range.
Foam	Excessive bather waste, including body oils, makeup, lotions, and detergents	Shock the water and bring sanitizer level into the proper range; add a defoamer.
	Total dissolved solids too high	Change the water.
Scum	Excessive bather waste, including body oils, makeup, lotions, and detergents	Use an over-the-counter tub and tile cleaner to scrub away the scum; use a scum-removal product.

TROUBLESHOOTING COMMON SPA PROBLEMS

Spas are designed to bring years of trouble-free enjoyment, but there is always that possibility that something might go wrong. Depending on the severity of the problem, you might be able to remedy the situation yourself. While a major problem with the equipment might require a service call to a spa professional, most water-quality issues probably can be handled by you. This section looks at the most common spa problems and what you can do about them. It begins with common water-related worries and moves on to more challenging equipment failures.

Water Worries

Itchy eyes, dry skin, cloudy water, and faded swimsuits are all symptoms of improperly balanced spa water. In fact, many spa water problems you might think are related to filtration are actually caused by poor water quality. Fortunately, routine water tests and the proper application of sanitizers and water-balancing chemicals (as described beginning on page 38) will keep your spa water sparkling and safe. Unfortunately, few spa owners have a perfect record of maintenance. And left unattended, spa water can quickly turn on you, presenting a litany of problems.

Never fear. Spa supply dealers carry a superfluity of chemicals to help you solve most any spa water crisis. If you're ever in doubt about which chemical to use, don't hesitate to ask your local spa supply professional. Most can analyze your water and prescribe just the remedy you're looking for. In no time at all, you'll be relaxing in your hot-water oasis, enjoying a perfectly balanced and germ-free spa.

Following are some of the more common chemicals you may encounter.

Algicides. These are used to kill algae and prevent them from taking root in your spa. Algae can grab hold of spa covers, pillows, and shells. It especially likes to lurk in tight corners where the water doesn't circulate well. It's important to make sure the algicide you use is designed to treat the type of algae you have. Some of the varieties include floating green algae, yellow/mustard algae, and black algae. The product label will tell you which kind of algae it's designed to eliminate. When applying an algicide, it may be necessary to use a stiff brush to expose all of the algae cells to the algicide.

Clarifiers. Also called flocculants, clarifiers herd small particles into clusters large enough to be caught by the spa's filtration system. Sequestering agents and chelating formulas are also clarifiers that keep metals and organic material, respectively, from coming out of solution so that they can't stain the pool or spa surface.

Defoamers. When certain algicides are used and/or pH is out of whack, the water begins to foam when agitated. This is a common problem with spas, which have blowers that introduce air into the water via the jets. For an immediate solution, add a few drops of defoamer to the water and allow it to circulate for several minutes. If the foam remains, add a few more drops. Repeat the process until the foam is gone. As a long-term solution to foaming, make sure the water is balanced, shock the water, and/or replace some of the water with fresh water.

Scum Removers/Preventers. Body oils, soaps, lotions, cosmetics, and other bather waste can accumulate on the water surface and cause blemishes around the spa's waterline, as well as in filter bays. This scum is rarely harmful, but it can be unsightly. Many over-the-counter tile cleaners will remove scum from spas, and spa supply dealers carry specialty chemicals for eliminating scum. To prevent scum from forming, have bathers shower before entering the spa. You can also use a scum-absorbing product that floats in the water and picks up scum before it has a chance to adhere to the spa walls.

Stain Removers. Stains are usually organic (caused by the tannins leaching out of plant debris that makes its way into the water) or metallic (caused by low pH, resulting in corrosive water that attacks the metals found in spa equipment and fittings). Stain removers will eliminate these unsightly blemishes.

Most water problems can be avoided if the water is properly balanced and sanitized. Some problems can be remedied only with specialty chemicals. However, if nothing you try seems to improve your water quality, simply drain the spa, clean the shell and the filter, and refill it with fresh water. There's no shame in starting with a clean tub of water.

Equipment Problems

Spa equipment has never been more durable. Nevertheless, equipment failures can occur. Sometimes it's difficult to pinpoint the problem, which can rest in the control panel, logic board, pump, motor, filter, plumbing, or automatic sanitizer. A skilled spa service professional, especially one trained in your particular brand of spa, should be able to get you up and running in no time.

If you can pinpoint the problem, however, you might be able to save some money on the service call. Most portable spas have a control panel that gives you a warning message when something is not right — from water temperatures that are too hot or too cold to malfunctions with the circulation system.

The owner's manual from your spa manufacturer will tell you what each warning message means and offer recommendations for fixing the problem. Here's a brief overview of spa filters, pumps, and heaters, along with some tips for solving the most common problems you may encounter.

SPA FILTERS

A spa filter removes impurities from the water much the same way that a lint trap collects fuzz in a clothes dryer. Without a filter, the water would be murky, cloudy, difficult to sanitize, and generally unsuitable for soaking.

The three possible types of filters for spas are sand, diatomaceous earth (DE), and cartridge. Most portable spas are built with integrated cartridge filters. In-ground spas may use any of the three filter types, each of which has its advantages and disadvantages. You should be familiar with all of them — especially if you have a custom spa — to make sure you're using the best filter for your particular setup. In general, DE costs the most but filters out the smallest particles. Sand costs the least but does the least effective job. Cartridges fall somewhere in the middle. Each filter type requires different maintenance procedures. However, because the vast majority of portable spas use cartridge filters, that's what we'll focus on here.

When something goes wrong with your spa's filtration system, water quality can deteriorate quickly. Poor filtration also leads to increased chemical costs and a greater need for sanitizer. Following are some basic cartridge filter problems and possible solutions. These guidelines are for general information only. Be sure to consult the owner's manual for your particular spa for specific recommendations and operating guidelines.

Cartridge Filter Problems

PROBLEM	CAUSE	SOLUTION
Flow rate is low.	Accumulated dirt is restricting water flow.	Clean the filter. (See pages 53–54.)
	There's an obstruction in the plumbing.	Locate and remove the obstruction.
	The pump impeller and diffuser are clogged or worn.	Clear any obstructions. Contact a service technician to replace worn parts.
Water needs to filter longer to maintain clarity.	The water is not balanced and/or the sanitizer residual is too low.	Balance the water and maintain the proper sanitizer residual. (See Spa Maintenance beginning on page 38.)
	The filter is undersized.	Make sure any new cartridge filters you install are the proper size for your spa.
	There's an unusual burden on the filter, caused by excessive dirt, debris, body oil, algae, or other contaminants.	Do your best to keep debris out of the water. Encourage bathers to shower before entering the spa.
	The filter isn't being cleaned properly.	Make sure you are following the manufacturer's guidelines for cleaning the filter. (See pages 53–54.)
Filtering is poor.	The sanitizer residual is low.	Maintain adequate sanitizer residual.
	The filter is too small, the flow rate is too low, and/or the operating time is too short to obtain an adequate turnover of the water.	Make sure the filter is properly sized and that there are no obstructions blocking the flow of water. Use the controls to extend filtration cycles.
	The filter isn't being cleaned properly.	Cartridge filters should be cleaned thoroughly whenever spa water is changed or more frequently if a lot of contaminants are allowed to enter the water. (See pages 53–54.) Follow manufacturer's guidelines.

SPA PUMPS

Spa pumps and motors are sold as a single integrated unit, so it's impossible to discuss one without the other. From here on out, when I say "pump," I'll mean the combined pump/motor. As a spa owner, you'll be happy to know that your pump requires little maintenance as long as it's been installed and operated properly. Nevertheless, the more you know about the pump, the more you'll appreciate it when it's functioning smoothly.

Portable spas are sold with equipment already installed, including the pump. To work effectively, a pump must be sized correctly for a particular spa size and jet configuration. Portable spa manufacturers have already done this for you. Problems can arise, though, if a pump needs to be replaced and the wrong size is installed. This can lead to excessive pressure in the system if the pump is too large or inadequate filtration if the pump is too small. Always refer to the owner's manual to determine the right size pump for your spa.

Most portable spas now include two-speed pumps, which can help save energy. The low speed is run during off-peak times to filter the water, and the high speed is used to power jets or to accelerate filtration during periods of high bather load. If you opt for a two-speed pump, make sure the low speed moves enough water for proper filtration.

Some units have multiple pumps and diverter valves to enable bathers to activate select jets. That way, one person can experience a hydromassage while another bather relaxes in less turbulent water.

Some spas also use a smaller pump that runs continually to circulate water through an automatic sanitizer and the heater to help

WATER IN MOTION

Spa pumps vary slightly in design depending on the manufacturer, but here is a look at a typical unit.

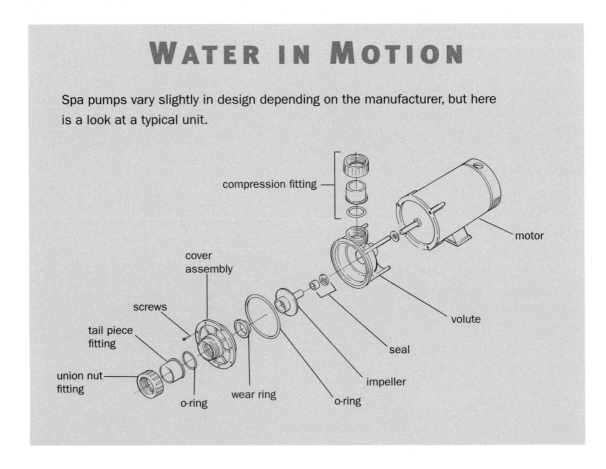

compression fitting

motor

cover assembly

screws

volute

tail piece fitting

seal

union nut fitting

impeller

o-ring

wear ring

o-ring

ensure that the water is ready 24 hours a day. Here are some things to keep in mind regarding pumps.

Priming. Always make sure that a spa is filled with water before activating the pumps; otherwise, the pump could lose its prime and the motor could overheat.

The Impeller. The pump body or volute holds the components of the pump, including the impeller. When the impeller spins, water or air is thrown out from the center by its vanes, which lowers pressure in the center and creates the pumping action. Rarely, small stones, grass, and other debris can plug the pump's impeller, impeding the flow of water. If that's the case, disassemble the pump and use a semirigid wire to clean the impeller.

The Seal. One other critical component of the pump is the mechanical seal that stops water from leaking out around the shafts between the pump and the electric motor. This mechanical seal is commonly a spring-loaded, rubber-cased unit, which is routinely replaced whenever the pump is professionally disassembled for other repairs. The seal itself uses ceramic and carbon parts. Ceramic and carbon seals are delicate and can be easily cracked if tapped with a screwdriver or other metal object. It's a good idea to know where the seal is and how to identify damage to it. If you determine that it needs to be replaced, call in a service professional; the disassembly of a pump and repair of worn or damaged seals is a job best left to a pro.

Installation. A portable spa cabinet with a louvered door is the ideal location for a pump — cool, clean, and dry so that dust, leaves, and other debris can't clog the motor's ventilation passages. When replacing a motor, make sure that it is elevated so that it doesn't come in contact with water puddles.

▲ When installing your spa, make sure that the panel to the equipment is accessible for regular maintenance and repairs.

Spa pumps and motors rarely fail, but when they do it can be for a variety of reasons, some common and others not so common. The following guide looks at some of the typical problems spa owners encounter. Keep in mind that pump and motor repair can be complicated; don't assume that you should undertake these repairs yourself. In fact, the warranty on the pump may become void if you tamper with the equipment yourself rather than having the work done by an authorized repair professional. Check your owner's manual for details.

If you believe you are qualified to make a repair, proceed with caution. Consult the manufacturer's literature, which often offers its own troubleshooting guide, and be sure to turn off the electrical power before getting to work.

Pump Problems

PROBLEM	CAUSE	SOLUTION
Pump won't run.	A circuit breaker is tripped or a fuse is blown.	Reset the breaker and/or replace the fuse. If the breaker trips or the fuse blows again, you may have an overloaded circuit, possibly caused by a short circuit in the motor.
	The motor has overheated.	If the thermal overload switch has been activated, reset it if there is a manual reset button. Keep in mind that something has caused the motor to over-heat, such as an obstruction in the inlet. Take the necessary steps to prevent it from happening again.
Pump loses prime.	The water level in the spa is low.	Raise the water level to the middle of the skimmer opening to prevent the pump from sucking air.
	The suction line has an air leak.	Tighten all pipes and fittings. Locate the leak, if any, and repair.
	The flange on the seal is improperly positioned.	Adjust the alignment.
	The seal on the pump is worn.	Check and replace if needed.
	The impeller is out of alignment.	Realign using an impeller gauge.
	The impeller is plugged.	Remove debris and other obstructions.
Pump leaks.	The seal or O-ring is defective.	Replace.
Water flows too slowly.	The filter is dirty.	Clean the filter as necessary.
	The impeller or diffuser is worn.	Replace.

PROBLEM	CAUSE	SOLUTION
Cavitation (air entering the circulation system) occurs.	Water level is too low.	Adjust water level.
	The circulation system is obstructed.	Check the lines on both sides of the pump and remove any obstructions.
Pump runs slowly.	The electric voltage is insufficient.	Use a voltmeter to check the voltage at the motor terminals and at the meter while the pump is running. If the voltage is low, consult the electric company to remedy the situation.
	An electrical connection is loose.	Disconnect the power and tighten any loose connections.
Motor hums but won't run.	The impeller is blocked.	Clear any debris from the impeller area. Spin the impeller and motor shaft by hand until it turns freely.
Motor runs but is noisy.	The bearings are worn.	Call a service technician. If you suspect worn bearings, it's important to have the repair done immediately, before more damage occurs. Some bearings are fitted with a plastic collar. If the motor is allowed to run with noisy bearings, they will eventually seize, melting the collar. Then the only solution is a new motor.
	The centrifugal switch spring has failed; the starter windings are burned out; or the motor is rusted or has insufficient lubrication.	These are complicated repairs best left to a service professional. Depending on the severity of the problem, a new pump may be necessary.

SPA HEATERS

Though there are several ways to heat water (gas, oil, solar, etc.), portable spa heaters are typically electric. In such units, heat is generated by an electric coil that either comes in direct contact with the water or wraps around a heat exchanger that transfers heat to the water. The immersed coil is more effective than the heat exchanger, but it's also more vulnerable to the corrosive effects of poorly balanced water. If you have an immersed coil heater and you don't keep your water properly balanced, the heater will eventually fail.

Portable spa manufacturers size heaters to provide fast and efficient operation. If you do need to replace one, make sure it's sized right for your particular spa. An undersized heater will heat too slowly, and an oversized heater will do the job but cost you more.

A heater's efficiency is determined by the percentage of British thermal units (Btu) of energy it is able to transfer to the water. No spa heater should be less than 75 percent efficient. In other words, for every 100 Btu produced by the heater, at least 75 Btu should be transferred to the water. Some high-efficiency heaters are able to transfer 95 percent or more. If you leave your spa uncovered when not in use, or the spa is subject to high winds, you may need a larger heater to achieve the desired temperature.

Also, you'll need to make a decision about continual versus intermittent use. A heater can be set to operate continually, ensuring that the water is at the desired temperature 24 hours a day, 7 days a week. If the heater is used only intermittently, that means you may need to wait for the water temperature to rise to a comfortable level before you get in your spa. Spa heaters can also be set to operate during filtration cycles, so the water temperature never drops very far below the desired temperature.

If you soak in your spa daily and at different times throughout the day, you'll want to maintain the temperature at a set point. If you soak only on weekends (maybe the spa is located at a weekend home or summer retreat), you'll want to heat the water only during those times. Keep in mind that it takes a lot more energy to raise the temperature of water several degrees than it does to maintain the higher temperature, but this cost may still be less than the cost to maintain a certain temperature at all times.

Heaters should be installed and serviced by trained professionals to make sure they're in proper working order. Let's take a look at some of the most common heating-related problems. You may be able to take care of some of these yourself; others will require a call to a service technician.

Electric Heater Problems

PROBLEM	CAUSE	SOLUTION
Heater won't heat water to desired temperature.	The heater isn't running long enough.	Extend the filtration/heating cycle.
	The filter is dirty.	Clean the filter.
	The thermostat is faulty.	Replace as needed.
	The heater is undersized.	Upsize heater as needed.
The water is too hot.	Thermostat is set too high.	Reduce thermostat setting.
	Filtration/heating cycle is too long.	Reduce filtration/heating cycle. (Even with the heater off, the water temperature can increase because the heat generated by the pumps is being transferred to the water.)
No heat is being generated.	Thermostat is not set high enough to switch on the heater.	Check and adjust the thermostat.
	The cover is off the spa and the heater can't compete with ambient air temperatures.	Keep the spa covered while it's heating.
	Heater is burned out.	Replace heater.

Saunas

3 Getting into Saunas

When it comes to exercise, a good sweat equals a good workout. Unless there are beads of sweat glistening on my brow, trickling down my back, and clinging to the tip of my nose, I don't feel like I'm making any progress.

The only thing that comes close to matching this feeling is time in a sauna. As soon as I enter one the sweat begins to flow. My skin is cleansed, my body is relaxed, and my mind is peaceful. It's no wonder that cultures throughout the world have made sweat baths an important part of their lives.

◀ A sauna is the perfect complement to a home gym. It helps loosen muscles before a workout and it soothes them after one.

SAUNA HISTORY AND CONTEMPORARY TRENDS

When envisioning the sauna lifestyle, people often conjure up images of robust Finns perspiring profusely on wooden benches while heat radiates from a bed of hot rocks. After a session in the sweat bath, the naked bathers run out of the sauna and plunge their glistening bodies into the chilly waters of a nearby lake or roll around in a fresh blanket of snow. As exotic as this may sound, it doesn't represent the modern-day reality of sauna use in the United States.

Though some sauna purists pooh-pooh anything other than a traditional wood-fired sauna fashioned from hewn logs, most of us are more familiar with contemporary saunas crafted from smooth cedar planks and warmed with an electric or gas heater. Instead of naked bodies sweating in unison, today's more modest sauna bathers are frequently wrapped in towels. And a cool shower is more likely to follow a sweat bath than a dip in frigid waters.

Indeed, sauna products and the lifestyle surrounding them have changed a great deal since the first sweat baths were created thousands of years ago for the Romans and Turks. Throughout history, civilizations around the world — from Native Americans to Asians — practiced some form of sweat bathing. In fact, many indigenous North Americans used some form of a sweat lodge. The Anishinabe of the Lake Superior region, for example, would heat stones on an open fire and then stack them on the floor of a small wigwam. The heated hut was typically used for therapy, as well as ceremonial and spiritual activities. Though many cultures enjoyed the concept of a sweat bath, it is the Finns who came to popularize the ritual and incorporate it fully into their day-to-day life.

▲ Sweat baths can be found in many cultures. Shown here is the interior of a Native American sweat lodge and healing hut.

The Finns deemed the sauna experience important to their health and happiness, and they used it with decorum. More than just a relaxing method of cleaning the body, the sauna was part of their social culture. For example, Finnish literature talks of a new bride dutifully preparing the sauna for her mother- and father-in-law and of the sauna being used to help one persevere through troubling times.

Frequently, rural neighbors took turns preparing the sauna for everyone to use at the end of a hard day in the fields. Also, it was common for women to give birth in the sauna. Supposedly, the tannic acid from the smoke sterilized the sauna surface, making it one of the few sanitary places to perform minor surgery or other medical procedures. In fact, a loose translation of an old Finnish proverb, "Sauna on köyhän apteekki," is "The sauna is a poor man's pharmacy."

Early Designs

In the 1800s the sauna resembled a small house made of logs. It was built tight with no exterior windows. Other than the door, the only opening was a small hole in the ceiling that allowed the smoke to get out. This hole was kept closed until the sauna was heated, typically by a wood fire built beneath a stone structure in the center of the room. Saunas were built away from other buildings in case they accidentally caught on fire. Once the desired temperature was reached, the fire was extinguished and women cleaned up the ashes and soot before shepherding everyone into the sauna.

A traditional sauna bath is taken in the nude — with men and women, children and adults, all enjoying the sauna together. After a few minutes in the intense heat, bathers often use birch switches to strike their backs, arms, and loins to promote circulation. Then water is poured over the body to clean and refresh it. To raise the sauna's temperature and to envelop bathers in temporary steam, water is ladled over the hot rocks. After about 30 minutes, bathers rinse themselves one last time and return to their homes to dress.

The sauna experience began to change in the late 1800s. Industrialization brought bathing conveniences into the home, and population growth made it more difficult for families to bathe simultaneously or to build saunas at a safe distance from other buildings. Meanwhile, new medical facilities usurped the role of saunas in childbirth and other health procedures. Finns even became less comfortable in their own skins, with both sexes modestly covering themselves when making their way to and from the sauna.

Changing times called for a changing sauna. Urban areas couldn't support the use of wood-fired saunas, which posed a fire threat to cities. But new heating technology wasn't available yet, causing sauna use to hit a historic low in the 1930s. World War II, however, ushered in a period of revitalization for the sauna industry. The depressed war economy offered few inexpensive entertainment options, and saunas offered a pastime most people could afford. Interestingly, during the war the military used tents equipped with sauna heaters to delouse soldiers and improve troop morale.

After the war the sauna industry intensified efforts to create a marketable sauna unit. Eventually, electric and gas-fired heaters were developed and manufactured, making saunas practical again for home use. Though other countries, such as Sweden and Germany, also began marketing their own saunas around this time, the Finns were reluctant to export a cultural icon. Even today, more than half of the world's saunas are in Finland, which boasts nearly as many saunas as cars, or about one sauna for every four people.

The first sauna in North America dates back to 1638 in Philadelphia and was erected by Finnish and Swedish immigrants who settled in the Delaware River Valley. In fact, some historians believe "Sauna" was the original name given to Philadelphia, where the first sauna was built on the site now occupied by the city hall.

During the late 1800s and early 1900s, Finnish immigrants came to America and settled in the Midwest — particularly Michigan, Wisconsin, and Minnesota — which offered a climate similar to Finland's. A sauna on the homestead, built in the traditional style of logs, stone, and mortar, made immigrants feel more at home in a foreign land. By some estimates, 90 percent of Finnish-American homesteads had a sauna — a higher percentage than in homesteads in Finland. These saunas were typically 8 by

15 feet (2.4 to 4.5 m) and constructed of squared logs. The saunas often included two rooms, one for dressing and one for basking. A lantern might hang in a window between the two rooms to illuminate both.

Explaining their bathing style to settlers from other countries, however, was difficult for Finnish immigrants. They had to overcome the hurdle of not only the language barrier but also the difference in attitudes. Some immigrants from other cultures viewed communal bathing as immoral. In 1920, for example, a Wright County, Minnesota, farmer brought suit against his Finnish neighbors in an attempt to force them to disband their use of a sauna as a "pagan temple." Fortunately, the judge sided with the Finns, who argued that the sauna was used for bathing, not pagan worship. He found the Finns to be law-abiding citizens with good Lutheran principles, and he ordered the plaintiff to pay the defendants $30 for slander.

During the first half of the 20th century, the Finnish sauna began making a name for itself in the United States. Finnish athletes, who performed on the world stage during Olympic competitions, extolled the benefits of sauna use. In the 1920s, just a few years after Finland had gained independence, one of the best-known Finnish athletes, Paavo Nurmi, nicknamed "The Flying Finn," dominated middle- and long-distance running, winning nine gold and three silver medals over the course of three Olympics. Since then, saunas and athletes have gone together like protein powder and health shakes.

In 1937, the Friends of the Finnish Sauna (later named the Finnish Sauna Society) was established to advocate the traditional Finnish sauna lifestyle. The members' work has paid off. As more people became familiar with and accepting of Finnish customs after the war, sauna sales began to increase,

▲ Though modern saunas are designed for luxury and convenience, some people still prefer rustic, wood-fired saunas for their authenticity.

spurred by the convenience of electric heaters. In the 1960s the media increased their coverage of the emerging popularity of saunas. In 1986, the sauna received its own day: the second Saturday in June.

Despite all the benefits of sweat baths, however, saunas still are not as popular as spas in the United States. According to the National Spa and Pool Institute, U.S. and Canadian hot tub manufacturers sold an estimated 387,000 hot tubs in 2003. That's 10 to 20 times more than the number of saunas sold. Nevertheless, more and more people are purchasing saunas. Some people are drawn to the high-temperature sweat bath experience, while others simply want to bring all of the amenities of a health club into their home. Though saunas can be installed outdoors like tradition would have it, it's much more common today for them to be placed indoors as part of a master bedroom suite or a home gym.

CHOOSING THE RIGHT SAUNA

If you're in the market for a sauna, you've probably experienced one in a health club or hotel gym. You remember how good you felt as your sweat flushed away toxins and your skin glowed from the intense heat. Unfortunately, a health club or hotel sauna isn't convenient every time you'd like to take a sweat bath. Plus, sharing the sauna with strangers detracts from the experience. As more people try to create a personal gym or health spa environment in their own homes, a sauna becomes a logical addition to a master bedroom or exercise area.

Embracing the sauna lifestyle is the first step in creating the perfect health spa environment for your home. Now that you've decided to make the investment, the question becomes, "What sauna should I buy?" The question sounds simple enough, but there are a lot of different types and styles to choose from, making the decision more complicated than you may have thought.

Original Finnish saunas were freestanding huts made of logs and heated with wood fires. They were built outdoors and could accommodate entire families and even some friendly neighbors. Today the vast majority of home saunas are small, two- to four-person units, although some are large enough to accommodate a dozen bathers. These contemporary saunas are warmed with electric heaters, allowing them to be built indoors or outdoors. Some are custom built to fit a particular space, while others are prefabricated and come in a variety of set sizes.

Another major point of differentiation is the style of heater. Most contemporary saunas use an electric heater that cooks a bed of rocks, which radiate an even and intense heat. Others use an infrared radiant heating system that is more localized and less intense,

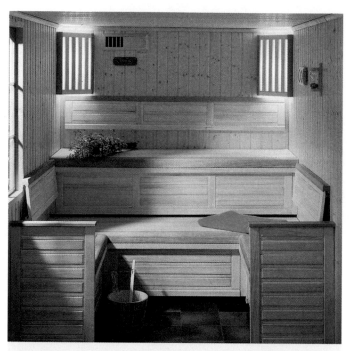

▲ The stereotypical sauna — a dark box relegated to the basement — is as passé as pet rocks and eight-track tape players. Today's saunas can be as stylish as you like. This one lets in natural light during the day and provides soft lighting for evening enjoyment. It also has banquet-style seating with contrasting wood trim and a complementary tile floor.

Today sauna manufacturers continue to do everything they can to make saunas more and more attractive to homeowners. For example, prefabricated units eliminate the need to construct a sauna from scratch. The addition of windows and glass doors makes people feel less claustrophobic. Infrared heaters provide instant and less intense heat for those who can't tolerate high temperatures. And mood lighting and CD players further enhance the sauna experience.

With technological advances in manufacturing and materials, there's no telling what saunas will look like 10 years from now. This much we can be sure of: Although saunas have a colorful history, they have an even brighter future.

PUTTING IT TOGETHER

Some small, prefabricated saunas are easy to put together. All components are preassembled, and each half of the sauna fits through a standard doorway. All that's left to do is to connect the two halves.

which appeals to people who don't like the superhigh temperatures of a more traditional sauna.

To help you navigate the sweltering sauna terrain, here's a brief discussion of the components that compose today's saunas.

The Room

Assuming you're not violating any building codes, you can opt for a traditional outdoor sauna fashioned from logs and heated by a wood fire. But you'll have to build it yourself or hire someone to do it. If you're looking for something more contemporary without the hassle of stoking a fire, then you'll want a sauna that resembles the ones you've experienced in hotels and health clubs.

Today's saunas are built from smooth, clear-grain softwoods such as cedar, Douglas fir, white spruce, and redwood. You can build your own sauna room with materials from a lumberyard, assuming that you're handy with tools and knowledgeable about woodworking techniques. Easier, however, is to purchase a prefabricated sauna, a precut custom sauna, or a custom sauna that uses tongue-and-groove construction.

Prefabricated. A prefabricated sauna is sold as a kit that you put together to make a freestanding unit. Typically, all of the walls and the ceiling are prebuilt panels that are finished on both sides. The panels should be insulated and include a vapor barrier to prevent the moisture in the sauna from getting into the room where the sauna is installed. Duckboard floor is often included, as well as a prehung door and all of the interior and exterior trim. As with a prefabricated spa, all of the necessary sauna equipment (heater, benches, controls, etc.) is included.

Precut Custom. A precut custom sauna kit includes all of the materials for a sauna designed to meet specific measurements. Instead of a freestanding unit, the sauna is attached directly to the framed, insulated walls of the main room. With a precut custom sauna, you can maximize your unique space. This may require you to frame additional walls, depending on the placement of the sauna and the design you choose.

Custom. A custom sauna is one that is entirely cut and built on-site. These are the most difficult to install for do-it-yourselfers because of all the carpentry work that is required. You'll have to frame and insulate walls before cutting boards to line the sauna. You'll want to use kiln-dried wood that hasn't been treated. The most common types of wood used are cedar, redwood, poplar, spruce, fir, and birch. Stay away from plywood, veneers, and hardwoods such as oak. You can also order custom pieces from a sauna manufacturer, but you'll need to build the room before submitting interior measurements for your sauna. If you don't want to undertake this project on your own, you can hire contractors to do a portion or all of the work.

PREFAB VS. PRECUT

There are advantages and disadvantages to both prefabricated and precut saunas. Following are some key factors to consider in making your selection.

	ADVANTAGES	DISADVANTAGES
Prefabricated Sauna	No carpentry skills required Fast assembly time Can be disassembled and moved	No ability to customize size or layout
Precut Sauna	Offers flexibility in planning and design Finished product looks like a custom-built sauna	Requires carpentry skills Can't be taken apart and relocated

HEATER OPTIONS

Freestanding Conventional Heater

Used for larger saunas

Wall-Mounted Conventional Heater

Used for smaller saunas

"Ever-ready" Conventional Heater

Used to eliminate heat-up time

Infrared Heaters

Placed on walls and below benches

The Heater

The sauna experience depends on the quality and type of heater used. In essence, the heater is the heart of the sauna — without it there is no warmth, and therefore no soothing and relaxing effects. Thus, it is of utmost importance that you choose the best heating system for your sauna.

The basic purpose of the sauna is to open the pores and encourage sweating. Not all heaters do this equally well or efficiently. There are two main types of sauna heaters: the traditional rock-style heater and the more inventive infrared heaters. Hard-core sauna advocates argue that a rock-style heater is the only way to enjoy an authentic

Finnish sauna. But several companies have succeeded in marketing infrared sauna heaters to consumers who simply want a dry, lower-temperature heat.

Traditional Rock Heaters. Traditional heaters use electricity, gas, oil, or wood. Encased in steel, these units are set on the floor or mounted to the wall. Small units are mounted to the wall for easier access and to allow the heat to disperse more evenly. When turned on, the heating element warms a bed of rocks, which then heats up the sauna through convection, much like an oven. It takes about 30 to 45 minutes for a traditional heater to achieve the desired temperature

▲ *Löyly,* the intense burst of humidity that makes the sauna feel hotter, is created by ladling water over the hot rocks.

range of 140 to 190°F (60 to 88°C). Fence the heater off to prevent bathers from coming in contact with the hot surface.

Most traditional sauna heaters require 220-volt electric service, although some smaller models plug into a standard 110-volt outlet. Though an electrician is needed to wire the sauna for 220-volt service, the heat-up time is dramatically faster than with the lower-voltage units.

Some newer models, however, are designed to eliminate waiting. These heaters use a large rock capacity and state-of-the-art insulating technology to keep the units ready. Bathers simply go into the sauna, open the heater lid, and enjoy immediate heat production. When not in use, these heaters typically consume the same amount of energy as a few lightbulbs. As an added bonus, these heaters usually don't need a safety fence because they boast a casing that remains cool due to the superior insulation. Though these models cost more than traditional sauna heaters, many homeowners believe the convenience of always having the sauna ready is worth the added expense.

A major advantage of traditional sauna heaters is that they enable you to customize your sauna environment — from hot and dry to high humidity. That's because a traditional sauna heater has lots of rocks that radiate an extremely hot, dry heat. If water is ladled over the rocks, steam is produced. This wave of soothing, moist heat, called *löyly,* envelops bathers like steam from a hot shower.

To offer an even broader range of sauna experiences, some heaters double as steam generators. These units operate like traditional sauna heaters, but they also include a steam generator that is plumbed to a water source. This allows you to create a much steamier environment than is possible by simply ladling water over the hot rocks.

Meanwhile, choosing the proper stones for your sauna heater is key. Heater manufacturers supply rocks ideally suited for sauna use, but you can also choose your own. Look for rocks with maximum strength and heat retention. The best rocks are igneous, which describes rock formed under conditions of intense heat or produced by the solidification of volcanic magma on or below the earth's surface. In this family of rocks are peridotite, olivine, and vulcanite. Before using your own rocks in your sauna heater, you should test them. One testing method is to get a fire going in an outdoor fire pit and place the rocks in the hot embers until the rocks heat up to at least 212°F (100°C). Retrieve them using metal tongs and plunge them into a bucket of cool water. After the rocks have cooled, inspect them for cracks, fissures, and breaks. You'll see that the rapid shift from extremely hot to cold temperatures will damage weaker stones. Some stones may contain minerals that release a bad odor when heated or wet, so check for unpleasant smells. Also, choose rocks that have a rough or uneven surface, because these will have more surface area, which helps produce better steam when water is ladled over them.

Infrared Heaters. Originally developed in the early 1970s for use in incubators, infrared heaters use a form of energy that is directly transmitted onto objects because of its specific wavelength. It has nothing to do with ultraviolet light, which can burn and damage skin. While traditional sauna heaters heat through convection, infrared heaters warm the body directly. Infrared heaters produce a dry, lower-temperature heat from a zirconium-tube energy source that heats the body from the inside out. Units generally warm up within 5 to 10 minutes and produce sauna temperatures of 110 to 150°F (43 to 66°C). Both 110-volt and 220-volt units are available. Though some people prefer the lower temperatures of infrared saunas, there is no way to introduce steam to create the *löyly* experience. Prefabricated infrared saunas are shipped with the right number of heaters preinstalled. If you are building your own, however, you should plan for about 17 watts for every cubic foot of sauna space. To determine the cubic footage, multiply the sauna length times the width times the height in feet. For example, a small personal sauna might be 4 feet long, 4 feet wide, and 6 feet tall. This means there are 96 cubic feet of sauna space ($4 \times 4 \times 6 = 96$). If you need 17 watts per cubic foot, you then would need 1,632 watts of heater energy ($17 \times 96 = 1,632$). If an infrared emitter provides 160 watts of

SOME LIKE IT HOT

Traditional sauna heaters heat rocks that radiate heat throughout the sauna. Water can be ladled over the rocks to create a burst of humidity, called *löyly*. Infrared heaters radiate less heat than traditional saunas. Several infrared heaters need to be placed throughout the sauna to create all-over heat.

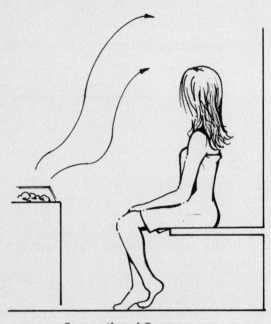
Conventional Sauna

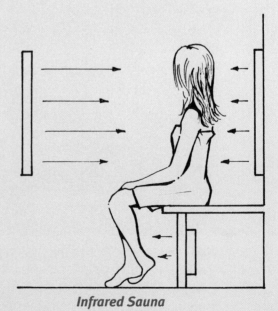
Infrared Sauna

energy, you would need about 10 emitters to heat the sauna (1,632 ÷ 160 = 10.2). Many manufacturers of infrared heaters include two or more emitters in each fixture.

Infrared saunas require the emitters to be placed all around bathers (behind, in front of, under the bench for the lower legs, and sometimes on the sides) so that bathers receive heat from all angles.

If you are unfamiliar with the two types of sauna heaters — traditional and infrared — be sure to test each kind. Sauna dealers typically allow customers to try out saunas before purchasing. For a realistic assessment, try out each sauna with little or no clothing on, just like you would if you were using it at home.

The Controls

Sauna controls are as simple to operate as a kitchen timer. Though they might be digital or mechanical, they all turn on the sauna

▲ Leg, head-, and back-rests make sauna bathing more comfortable.

heater and allow you to set the duration of operation. Most sauna heaters include a thermostat that allows you to set a maximum temperature. Some digital controls will display the actual temperature so you can check the progress — sort of like preheating an oven. For mechanical controls that don't display the actual temperature, you'll need to install a thermometer inside the sauna.

If your sauna is equipped with interior lighting, you can purchase a control panel that includes a light switch. Also, some digital controls display the time, tell you how many minutes remain on the timer, and enable you to program the heater to come on at a specific time. At least one manufacturer offers a digital control that remembers the amount of time needed to reach a desired set temperature so that you can better plan future sauna use.

Traditional heater manufacturers often include controls that are right on the heater, but ancillary controls are frequently installed on the sauna's exterior wall as well for convenience. Oftentimes you have a choice of finishes, such as white, chrome, brass, nickel, and gold, so that it's possible to coordinate the look with other fixtures and furnishings in the room.

The Benches

Saunas need upper and lower benches. The upper bench, called *laude* in Finnish, is necessary to take advantage of the sauna heat, which rises to the ceiling. The lower bench is needed to step up to the upper bench, as well as to enjoy the lower temperatures toward the floor of the sauna.

Benches must be deep enough to accommodate all body types. As a guideline, upper benches should be at least 20 inches (50 cm) wide, and lower benches should be about

▶ This sauna is equipped with a television monitor and speakers, so there's never a need to choose between basking and TV entertainment.

16 inches (40 cm) wide. Remember, a sauna with cut corners and angles reduces the amount of usable bench space you can fit inside. You'll need benches that are at least 6 feet (1.8 m) long if you intend to lounge. For greater comfort, consider adding wooden headrests and leg rests.

If you are building your own sauna, it is important that you don't build benches (or walls) in such a way that the heads of nails and screws are exposed to bathers. The metal will get extremely hot and can burn skin.

Other Amenities

Saunas have evolved more in the past few decades than they have in the previous millennium. To appeal to a broader audience of consumers, manufacturers have adapted the sauna to address the reasons some people are "turned off" by saunas.

Today's saunas are available with glass doors and windows to create a more open feeling. Mood lighting is common to enhance nighttime enjoyment for those who don't like the dark. And interior speakers are popular for bathers who relax better with music.

Other accessories that enhance the sauna experience run from the practical to the purely pampering. They include thermometers, hygrometers, wooden buckets and ladles, sand timers, aromatherapy oils, mat flooring, towel pegs, and body brushes to promote circulation.

As you can see, you must make a lot of decisions before purchasing the ideal sauna for you and your family. But once you've determined the type of sauna and accessories you want to include, you can begin the fun and exciting task of designing your ultimate sauna environment.

THE 7-FOOT SAUNA

The ideal height for a sauna is about 7 feet (2.13 m). This ensures that the sauna heats efficiently and that the heat stays where the bathers are. This diagram shows how to construct a wall that will yield an interior sauna height of 7 feet (2.13 m).

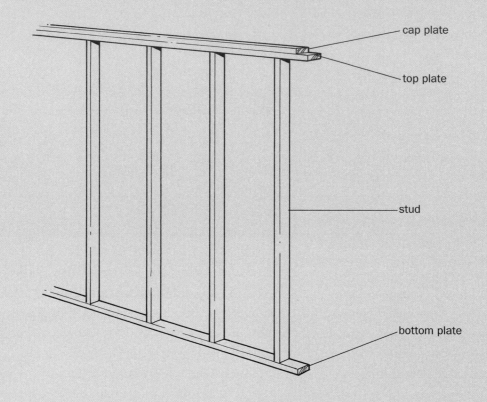

WALL COMPONENT	HEIGHT
2 x 4 bottom plate	1.5 inches (3.8 cm)
2 x 4 studs	80.0 inches (2 m)
2 x 4 top plate	1.5 inches (3.8 cm)
2 x 4 cap plate	1.5 inches (3.8 cm)
	Total Height = 84.5 inches* (2.15 m)

* With the ceiling boards attached, the finished height will drop to 84 inches (2.13 m), or 7 feet (2.13 m). To make the sauna taller or shorter, simply adjust the length of the studs accordingly.

PLANNING AND DESIGNING THE SAUNA ENVIRONMENT

The best time to plan a sauna is when you are building a house. That way you can design the sauna into the master plans. But most of us develop our interest in saunas well after we have settled in, so the challenge for us is to seamlessly incorporate a sauna into our existing abode.

That task has been made much easier thanks to the wide range of sauna sizes and styles offered today. But before you go shopping for a sauna kit or raw materials, you'll need to plan your installation carefully to make sure the end result is everything you hoped it would be. The simplest way to go about it is to ask yourself a series of key questions. These are among the considerations you'll need to address:

● *What type of sauna do you want?* The previous section discussed the differences between prefabricated and custom-built saunas, as well as the differences between traditional and infrared heaters. Heater performances differ greatly, so you'll want to make sure to test each one to determine which experience you prefer.

● *How big should your sauna be?* You want to keep the sauna as small as possible to achieve the greatest heating efficiency. At the same time, you want to ensure that it's large enough for ultimate relaxation and enjoyment. That means having adequate room for both sitting and reclining. A rule of thumb is to allow 2 feet (60 cm) of bench space per person for sitting. For reclining, you'll need a bench that is at least 6 feet (1.8 cm) long.

● *What shape will it be?* Most saunas are square or rectangular. But sometimes it's desirable to have a sauna with cut corners and angles instead of 90-degree corners. For example, such designs work well in tight areas where you have limited space for the door to open and people to maneuver around the sauna. However, realize that irregularly shaped designs often greatly reduce the amount of usable bench space you'll be able to include.

● *How will the benches be positioned?* If you want to take advantage of the higher temperatures toward the ceiling, you'll want to install an upper bench.

● *Will the sauna have windows?* Though a sauna won't heat as well with windows, it's often nice to incorporate one or two into your

▲ Though glass walls and doors make it more difficult to heat a sauna, they create an open atmosphere in what otherwise might feel like a dark closet.

SAUNAS FOR EVERY SIZE

Whether you're looking for an intimate two-person sauna or one that can hold a bachelor party, there's a sauna for you. Prefabricated and precut saunas come in set sizes, but you can order custom-cut saunas to fit your space perfectly.

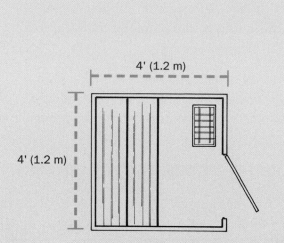

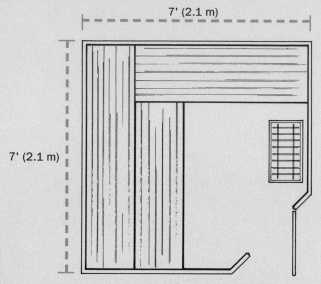

▲ A small, two-person sauna may fit nicely in a master bedroom or bathroom.

▲ A cut-corner design makes it easier to walk around a sauna, especially one that's tucked into a corner.

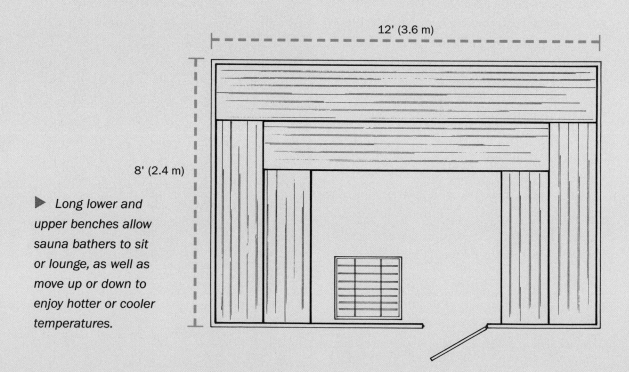

► Long lower and upper benches allow sauna bathers to sit or lounge, as well as move up or down to enjoy hotter or cooler temperatures.

design to let in natural light, take in a lovely view, or merely make the room seem less enclosed. Sauna doors with glass panes can be purchased to simplify the task of incorporating windows.

● *Where will you install the sauna?* A sauna can be put anywhere you have space, inside or outside. All you need is a waterproof floor and electrical service. Outdoor saunas can be placed on decks and patios, as well as next to lakes, ponds, and swimming pools. Indoor saunas are perfect accompaniments to a master bath, a bedroom suite, a home gym, a solarium, a garage, and even a basement.

● *Will you have any adjacent facilities?* If you have the extra space, consider including a changing room with a cool-down bench. This is especially nice if your sauna is being installed outside. It's also recommended that you have a shower nearby for convenient showering before and after a sauna bath.

● *What type of wood will you use?* Softwoods work better than hardwoods, which can become excessively hot and brittle over time. Also, certain softwoods have wonderful aromas that add to the ambience. Two of the best woods to consider are clear cedar and aspen. Other good possibilities include hemlock, redwood, spruce, fir, and birch. However, stay away from plywood, veneers, and sap wood; the latter comes from the outer part of the tree and carries the sap. Whatever wood you use, it should be kiln-dried so that the moisture content is no more than 10 percent. This will prevent shrinkage and warping. Also, don't use boards with knots, which can retain excessive heat and scorch bathers.

● *What type of construction will you use?* The best way to create a tight fit and prevent the wooden interior from warping is to use tongue-and-groove construction on the walls

▲ Most prefabricated and precut saunas use wall boards that run vertically.

and ceiling. Square-edged boards should be avoided because they do not form a smooth, sealed surface where the boards meet. With tongue-and-groove assembly, you simple nail the "tongue" at an angle and then cover it up with the "groove" of the next board. It's a good idea to check the boards with a level every so often to make sure you're staying on track. When constructing walls and benches, it's important not to have any nail or screw heads showing, which can heat up and brand unsuspecting bathers. (For diagrams of custom sauna wall and bench construction, see the facing page.)

● *Should the boards run vertically or horizontally?* This is a matter of personal preference, although you'll find that most prefabricated and precut saunas are designed with the boards running vertically from the floor to the ceiling.

SOME ASSEMBLY REQUIRED

If you're thinking of purchasing a prefabricated or precut sauna, it's important to know what's included in the deal. A prefabricated sauna comes with framed and insulated walls and requires minimal assembly. A precut sauna comes in standard or custom sizes and requires more labor. Even though the precut boards are already sized and labeled for assembly, you still need to frame and insulate the walls. If you're ordering a custom sauna, it's best to do all of your framing first and then take your measurements to ensure a perfect fit.

A materials list for a precut sauna kit includes:

- *Tongue-and-groove boards* for the walls and ceiling

- *Materials for two-tiered benches,* including fascia boards, stiffeners, crosspiece supports, and screws for bottom fastening

- *Duckboard floor* to cover the open part of the floor in front of the benches

- *Heater and controls*

- *Heater rocks*

- *Heater guard,* if necessary, to protect bathers from accidental contact

- *Door,* with or without a window, and related hardware

- *Light fixture,* which should be vapor-proof and rated for sauna use

- *Foil vapor barrier*

- *Finishing nails*

Some precut saunas also include an accessory kit (thermometer, water bucket, ladle, aromatherapy oils, etc.). The materials not typically included are 2 x 4 framing for walls, insulation, air grills for ventilation, wiring, and exterior paneling or wall covering.

◀ *Precut saunas come with all the pieces you'll need to assemble and enjoy your own sauna.*

With vertical boards, moisture has an easier time running down to the floor. Horizontal boards, in contrast, can trap moisture in the grooves, which can lead to wood stains.

Vertical board construction can be more expensive because all the boards need to be the full height of the sauna, whereas horizontal construction allows the use of shorter boards on narrower walls.

With horizontal construction, every row must be cut to length; with vertical construction, you can purchase 7-foot (2.1 m) lengths to cover the floor-to-ceiling distance and avoid cutting. Only the last board on each wall would need to be ripped to fit width.

The biggest drawback to vertical construction — and it's really pretty minor — is that you'll have to install horizontal strapping every foot (30 cm) around the framed 2 × 4 walls so that you have something to attach the boards to. If you want to gain an inch around the inside perimeter, you can opt to install horizontal blocks between the studs instead. Of course, this is not an issue with prefabricated saunas, which include the walls already assembled.

● **How will the heater be installed?** Your heater must be sized to accommodate the cubic footage of your sauna. Some wall heaters are small and lightweight enough to be attached directly to the tongue-and-groove boards. Heavier units with a large rock capacity need to be mounted to the studs behind the boards. If you have to attach the heater to the studs, be sure to plan carefully and install extra studs if necessary so you can place the heater exactly where you want it. Another option is to use a floor-standing heater.

● **How will the door be installed?** Sauna doors should open outward from the sauna and should not be equipped with any latching device requiring lifting or turning to exit the sauna. A good option is a roller latch that allows the door to be opened merely by pushing or leaning on it. Also, plan whether you want the door to swing to the left or the right, which will depend on your particular setup.

● **Will there be a light in the sauna?** Lighting can make the sauna more inviting, but it must be waterproof and certified for use in a sauna. If a fixture doesn't meet these criteria, don't use it, no matter how much you like it. Plan to install the light away from the benches so it doesn't interfere with bathers. Some prefabricated saunas have recessed lights under the benches or in soffits around the ceiling, which produce a soft glow.

● **Will you need to prep the walls and ceiling before installation?** Prefabricated saunas are finished on all sides and are designed to stand alone like a piece of furniture. Precut and custom saunas, however, are attached directly to walls of your home. Note that you cannot build a sauna over existing drywall. Over time, moisture from the sauna will damage the drywall. Therefore, be sure to remove all drywall from the walls and ceiling. Make sure that there is adequate insulation between the studs, and cover the wall and ceiling completely with a foil vapor barrier, which reflects heat back into the sauna and prevents moisture from getting into the walls of your home. Though you want to prevent moisture damage and heat loss, keep in mind that a sauna should not be airtight. In fact, it's important to have adequate ventilation that continually brings fresh air into the sauna. But if you're having difficulty maintaining your sauna's temperature, you might be exchanging the air too quickly. Through trial and error you'll create the perfect rate of air exchange for your specific sauna.

INSTALLING TONGUE-AND-GROOVE BOARDS

Custom-made saunas — whether precut to your specifications by a manufacturer or made from scratch by you — allow you to build a sauna that perfectly matches your space and desired configuration. Walls, framed with 2 × 4s, should be insulated and covered with a foil vapor barrier before you install the tongue-and-groove boards. Boards installed horizontally can be attached directly to the wall studs. Vertical boards must be attached to wood strapping that has been nailed to the studs every 12 inches (30 cm).

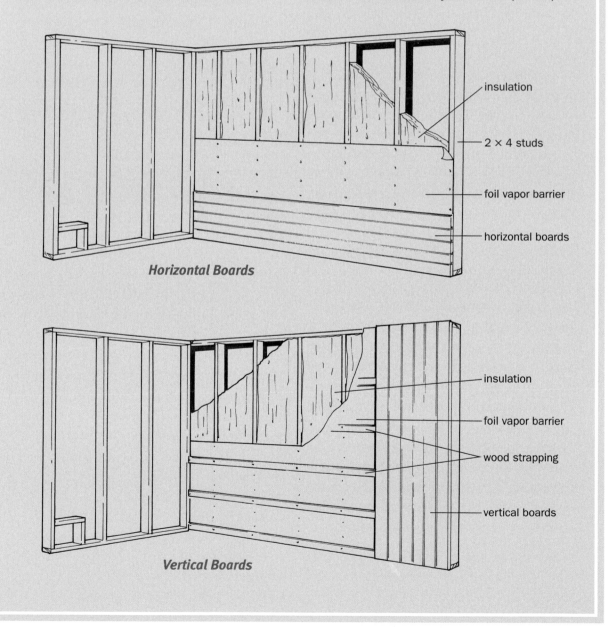

insulation

2 × 4 studs

foil vapor barrier

horizontal boards

Horizontal Boards

insulation

foil vapor barrier

wood strapping

vertical boards

Vertical Boards

• *What type of floor surface will you use?* In original outdoor Finnish saunas, the floor was dirt with maybe a few wooden planks on the ground for people to walk on as they made their way toward the benches. Today outdoor sauna designs typically include a duckboard floor. You can also install a sauna directly over concrete or a wooden deck.

For indoor saunas, the floor beneath the duckboards must be waterproof so that it can be cleaned easily and isn't susceptible to water damage. A concrete floor (such as in the basement) works well. This can be dressed up with either duckboards or plastic draining mats. Tile is becoming increasingly popular because of its upscale look and ease of maintenance. Whatever material you choose, it should be able to stand up to the climate inside a sauna.

• *Should you install a drain?* Your sauna does not *require* a drain. Most of the water poured on the rocks is turned into steam. (Note: Use only potable water, not water from a swimming pool or hot tub, which may contain corrosive chemicals and be unhealthy to breathe when it becomes aerosolized.) Any small amount of water that does land on the floor can be wiped away or left to evaporate. However, if you are building your sauna from scratch and have the budget for plumbing, you might want to consider installing a drain, which will enable you to clean your sauna more easily.

• *How tall will the sauna be?* Remember that heat rises, so you don't want the sauna any taller than it has to be. Seven feet (2.1 m) enables most people to stand comfortably inside while keeping most of the heat at a level where bathers sit. If you have high ceilings in your house, you can leave the space above the sauna open, use it to display art objects, or build in storage cabinets.

• *Is there easy access to electricity?* Some small saunas can be heated with a modest 110-volt heater, but most will require special 220-volt service. Work with an electrician to determine how a 220-volt line will be run to your sauna. You might decide to relocate the sauna if your original spot is too hard to reach.

By considering these questions, you'll be well on your way to designing the perfect sauna for you and your family. Nevertheless, you'll definitely want to visit some sauna showrooms before making your final decision. A sauna that looks good on paper has a totally different feel when you actually get inside. By visiting a sauna dealer and testing a variety of sizes and styles, you'll have a better idea of what you really want.

▲ Ideally, there should be a place to relax and rehydrate between sauna innings.

Getting the Most Out of Saunas

So many things in life make us feel good, but science hasn't always been able to explain why. A tender hug from a child. A handmade kite in flight. Overhearing somebody compliment us — especially when we're supposed to be out of earshot. The warm, sweet smell of freshly baked cookies. And, of course, time spent in a sauna. "If only we could bottle them," people say of these wonderful sensations. "Then we could enjoy them whenever we want to." Indeed, the ability to improve one's physical, emotional, and psychological well-being on demand would be a splendid thing.

◀ An "ever-ready" conventional heater remains warm at all times to reduce the heat-up time. This model can be controlled by a hand-held remote so bathers need not exit the sauna to adjust the thermostat or timer.

So imagine my joy when I heard that researchers from Oklahoma State University had found evidence that sweat therapy is an effective way to improve mental well-being. "The heat of a sauna or sweat lodge is a dynamic force," researcher Stephen Colmant said at a 2003 meeting of the American Psychological Association. "Group sweating has had a central place in societies through-out the world for thousands of years in helping people gain more physical, mental, and spiritual health."

In short, Colmant and his colleagues examined the way 24 participants responded to counseling. One group received just counseling, and the other received counseling along with group sweat therapy in a 145°F (63°C) sauna. The sauna group reported more relaxation, stress relief, and a feeling of accomplishment from having sweated it out. They also found their counseling to be more beneficial, and they got along better with other members of their group. According to the researchers, this suggests that there is an impact on a person's mental well-being that occurs with physiological changes.

I have always thought it was impossible to be mad at or to fight with someone while enjoying a sauna together. Now I have discovered that science backs me up.

SAUNA ENJOYMENT AND SAFETY

In Finland, learning how to take a sweat bath is as natural as learning how to dress. Yet, as with dressing, there is no single "right way" to enjoy a sauna bath. Each person has his or her own way of approaching the matter, and no one should ever claim that his or her way is superior to all others. There are many techniques and rituals associated with sweat baths, and all of them are acceptable.

▲ Research has shown that sauna use is an effective way to improve mental well-being.

The key to having a pleasurable sauna experience is to listen to your body and follow your own rhythm in moving in and out of the sauna and alternating between the top and bottom benches. Some competitive individuals — mostly men — approach the sauna bath like an endurance sport that's won by proving that they can withstand the scalding sauna temperatures longer than anyone else. But wiser sauna enthusiasts will quietly slip out of the sauna when they feel the need for a break and have a drink of water while cooling down on a comfortable bench or chaise lounge.

It's important to set aside enough time to become fully engaged in the sauna experience. The sauna is no place for anyone in a hurry. It's not like taking a quick hot shower in the morning before throwing on some clothes and dashing out the door so that you're not late for work. Rather, the sauna is best enjoyed in the evening or when you have a couple of hours to fully relax. The Finns, for example, pride themselves on making the sauna a part of their evening entertainment, complete with conversation, drinks, and maybe a light dinner.

SAUNA SAFETY

Though saunas offer a wealth of health benefits, they can also cause harm if used incorrectly or by people with certain health problems. Until you are familiar with how your body responds to sauna use, it's best to err on the side of caution and follow these safety guidelines.

- *Basic safety precautions should be followed* when installing and using sauna electrical equipment. Don't attempt to hard-wire your sauna heater unless you're a licensed electrician. The main control panel must be installed in a dry place outside the sauna.

- *Use a ground fault circuit interrupter (GFCI)* if the sauna is being placed in a wet location, such as outside or in a bathroom. A licensed electrician should know what the GFCI code requirement is in your area, but it's something you should still ask him or her about.

- *Install a guardrail around the heater* according to the heater manufacturer's guidelines, and do not place combustible material on the heater at any time.

- *Don't include any locking or latching system* on the door of the sauna to prevent the possibility of entrapment.

- *Don't allow children to use the sauna* unless they are supervised at all times by a responsible adult.

- *Make sure that the sauna is vented* to ensure an adequate supply of fresh air. In a residential sauna, the air should be changed about six times an hour. The proper way to vent the sauna is to place a 2- to 3-inch (5 to 7.5 cm) vent beneath the heater on the adjacent wall to bring in fresh air. Another vent should be placed along the ceiling to allow air to exit.

- *Pregnant or possibly pregnant women should avoid sauna use* until they get the okay from their physician, who can tell them what temperature of sauna use is safe. High temperatures have the potential to cause fetal damage, especially during the early months of pregnancy.

- *Don't use the sauna immediately after performing strenuous exercise.* To prevent overheating, wait until your body has cooled completely before entering the sauna.

- *If you have been drinking excessively, avoid sauna use altogether.* If you are taking prescription medication, consult your physician before using the sauna, because some medications may induce drowsiness and affect heart rate and blood pressure. Alcohol, recreational drugs, and medications may affect your body's ability to withstand sauna temperatures and could cause you to lose consciousness.

● *Consult a physician prior to using a sauna* if you suffer from obesity, heart disease, low or high blood pressure, circulatory system problems, or diabetes.

● *Exit immediately if you feel uncomfortable, dizzy, or sleepy.* Staying too long in a sauna can cause you to overheat and develop hyperthermia. Hyperthermia occurs when the internal temperature of the body reaches a level several degrees above normal. The symptoms of hyperthermia include dizziness, lethargy, drowsiness, and fainting. The effects of hyperthermia include failure to perceive heat, failure to recognize the need to exit the room, unawareness of impending hazard, fetal damage in pregnant women, physical inability to exit the room, and/or unconsciousness.

● *Exercise caution when entering and exiting the sauna.* For example, you might trip over a threshold or slip on a tile floor.

● *Never sleep inside the sauna* while it is operating. You may not awake before hyperthermia sets in.

● *Replace damaged electrical cords immediately.* Turn off the power at the breaker switch and have the cord replaced by a licensed electrician.

● *Do not use an outdoor sauna during an electrical storm,* as there is a remote chance of being hit by lightning.

● *Dry your hands before adjusting electrical controls.* The potential for electrical shock exists.

Sauna Benefits

The sauna provides a therapeutic environment that improves mental and physical health. The combination of perspiring, resting, and then cooling stimulates circulation, reduces muscular pain, and can lessen nervous tension. Here are some other benefits of using a sauna:

● *Soothes and relaxes tired muscles.* Many sauna users, including those with back pain, experience physical rejuvenation. Sauna bathing can also help relax muscles before and after a workout.

● *Lessens anxiety.* Some people maintain that after leaving the sauna, their mind is more relaxed, lucid, and free from day-to-day worries. When the body feels soothed and energized, the mind and emotions often follow suit.

▲ Since their advent, saunas have been a place for family relaxation and bonding.

● *Helps relieve arthritic pain.* Like hot tubs, saunas supply heat that makes it easier for people with arthritis to bend afflicted joints.

● *Relieves cold symptoms.* Saunas reduce congestion, as well as allergy symptoms.

● *Cleanses skin.* When the body sweats, pores in the skin open up and unhealthy toxins are flushed out. Some sauna users believe this gives them a healthier, more youthful complexion. At a minimum, sweating promotes a wonderful feeling of well-being.

● *Improves shaving.* The heat and sweat of the sauna open pores and soften hair follicles, making it easier to get a close shave.

● *Promotes better sleep.* A sauna bath relaxes the body and leads to a more restful sleep. However, make sure that you allow enough time to cool down before getting into bed.

● *Provides aromatherapy.* When used with essential oils such as eucalyptus, the sauna doubles as an aromatherapy chamber. If you decide to use an essence or fragrance, do not add it directly to the rocks. These fragrances are concentrated and need to be diluted in water first. The water can then be ladled over the rocks when creating *löyly*. Be sure to read all instructions and warnings supplied by the fragrance manufacturer before using it in your sauna.

● *Bonds a family.* When family members enjoy a sauna together, they often engage in the most meaningful conversations of the day, which is worth a great deal in this day and age when it's often nearly impossible to coordinate family schedules.

● *Increases home value.* In many instances, the addition of a permanent sauna in your home will be appraised for more than you originally spent on it.

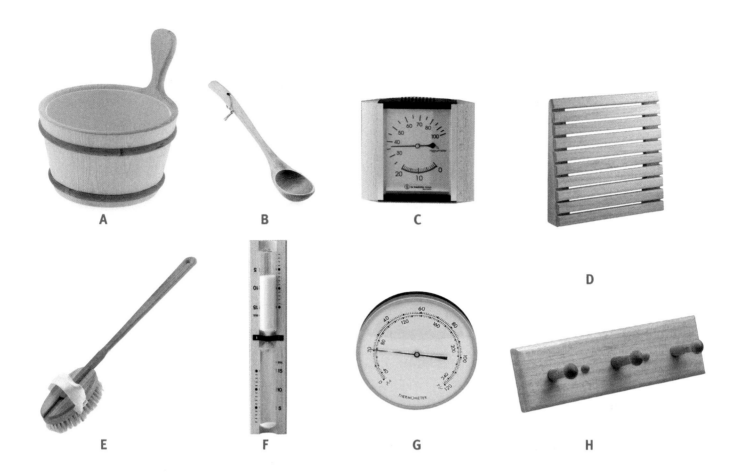

Sauna Accessories

Now that you know the benefits of taking a sauna bath, you'll be excited to learn that there are some key accessories that enhance the experience. They aren't absolutely necessary, but they contribute greatly to the sauna decor and lifestyle. Complete your sauna setting with the following:

● *Bucket (A),* used to hold water for splashing on the sauna rocks

● *Long-handled ladle (B),* used with the bucket to safely splash water on the rocks without getting burned by the heater and rising steam

● *A birch whisk,* or *vihta,* used to swat the skin to promote blood circulation

● *Sauna thermometer (C),* for observing changes in the sauna temperature

● *Wooden headrests, backrests, and leg rests (D),* which provide personal comfort

● *Mild sauna soap,* not for use in the sauna, but designed for showering after the sauna

● *Scrub brushes and loofah sponges (E),* used for washing

● *Sand timers (F),* for keeping track of time spent in the sauna

● *Hygrometers (G),* for measuring humidity in the sauna

● *Aromatherapy oils,* for mixing with the water that's thrown on the rocks

● *Wooden pegs (H),* for hanging clothes and robes in the dressing area or alongside the sauna

● *Large, luxurious towels,* perfect for absorbing moisture and protecting the sauna bench

FIRING UP YOUR NEW SAUNA

After you've installed your new sauna, you must take several steps before you can enjoy your first sweat bath. This procedure is called "curing" the sauna, and it's simply a matter of cleaning the unit and heating it to break in the wood.

1 **CLEAN UP.** Remove all packing and construction materials, and vacuum the entire interior to remove sawdust and debris. Wipe down all of the woodwork with a damp cloth.

2 **PREPARE THE HEATER ROCKS.** First, wash the rocks in a bucket until the water runs clear. Then place the rocks in the heater. Pile them loosely. If you install the rocks too densely, air won't be able to flow through the heater and rocks efficiently. The heater could overheat and trigger the high-limit switch. If this happens, you'll need to let the heater cool before repositioning the rocks and resetting the switch.

3 **FIRE UP THE SAUNA.** Double-check to make sure all of the electrical connections are secure. Then operate the heater for about 20 minutes to burn off the manufacturer's coating on the elements. The sauna might smoke and smell for a few minutes, but this is normal.

4 **CURE THE WOOD.** Operate the sauna at its highest temperature for an hour with the door closed. Don't allow anyone in the sauna during this time. After an hour, slowly pour about a quart (1 liter) of water on the rocks to steam-clean them and complete the final stage of the curing process. If water is dripping on the floor before it can turn into steam, you

are pouring too quickly. Occasionally, a rock may crack or break under this stress test. After the rocks have cooled completely, discard any broken ones.

5 **ENJOY.** Now your sauna is primed and ready to go. Simply throw down a towel and relax in the soothing warmth of your sweat bath retreat.

 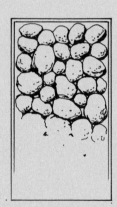

Correct placement
of sauna rocks

Overpacked
sauna rocks

▲ *Sauna rocks should be placed in the heater so that air is free to circulate among them. Overpacking the rocks can cause the unit to overheat, thereby triggering the high-limit temperature device. Before loading the rocks, verify that the heater is securely mounted to the wall or floor, and make sure the heater is off and cool.*

How to Take a Traditional Sauna Bath

There is no one right way to take a sauna bath. But that won't prevent me from offering recommended procedures to the novice or uninitiated sauna users. Here are some guidelines for taking a traditional sauna. Saunas heated with infrared fixtures can't produce steam, but all of the non-heater-related recommendations will work for these saunas, too. Before taking your first sauna, however, check with your physician to make sure the intense heat won't be a health risk.

STEP 1. *Reserve enough time* — at least an hour, preferably two. Unless your sauna has a heater that's constantly on, you'll need about 30 minutes to heat up the rocks.

STEP 2. *Undress and take a shower* to remove any body oils, lotions, hair products, makeup, deodorants, and other contaminants you don't want in the sauna.

STEP 3. *Enter the sauna,* placing a towel on the bench before sitting or reclining. A traditional sauna is taken in the nude. But feel free to wrap a towel around yourself or don a bathing suit.

STEP 4. *Sit back for a few minutes and let the heat permeate your body* and open the pores in your skin. The air may feel stiflingly dry at first. If that's the case, you can adjust the air moisture by ladling water onto the stones of the heater. The steam will make the room feel hotter, but not so dry. (Caution: Do not put water on infrared sauna heaters!) If this is your first time in a sauna, start with the temperature at about 176°F (80°C) and increase the temperature as you desire. (Note: Infrared-heated saunas operate at lower temperatures.) If you want a hotter experience, move to the upper bench, where the heat rises. For a cooler experience, move to the lower bench or let some of the heat out the door.

STEP 5. *After 10 to 20 minutes, or if you start to feel too hot, leave the sauna* and cool off by taking a shower, jumping in a pool, swimming in a lake, rolling in the snow, or just lounging. Check with your doctor before trying some of the extreme methods of cooling down to make sure your body can handle the shock. Whatever method you choose, be sure to have a cool drink to replenish fluids, but avoid alcohol, which can dehydrate you even more and impair your judgment.

▲ In a traditional sauna, bunches of tender birch branches, or *vihta,* are used to gently swat the body and promote circulation.

STEP 6. *After cooling off, return to the sauna.* After you warm up again, use a *vihta* to promote circulation. The *vihta*, a whisk made of supple young birch twigs tied together, is used to gently or robustly swat the body from head to foot. Traditionally, the birch twigs are harvested in the spring, and some *vihta* devotees freeze them for use year-round. They are easily "revived" by soaking them in warm water. The smell of birch leaves is so synonymous with saunas that some companies make birch-scented soaps and shampoos.

If you don't have access to a real *vihta*, you can opt for a wooden whisk, available from sauna dealers. Many people think the whisk provides a more pleasant experience than brushing or scrubbing. In either case, make sure that your skin is sufficiently supple and moist before you start swatting yourself senseless.

STEP 7. *Cool off again.*

STEP 8. *Repeat the sauna sessions as often as you'd like,* although two innings are sufficient for most people. However, it's comforting to warm up in the sauna one last time before taking a shower.

STEP 9. *Shower, dry off, put on a robe,* get a nonalcoholic drink, and recline with your eyes closed until you feel cooled down. If you don't allow enough time to cool off before dressing, you may continue to sweat in your clothes. Also, a sauna can dry out your skin, so you might want to apply a moisturizing lotion before getting dressed.

These steps make up just one set of guidelines. Enjoying a sauna is a personal thing, and you will develop your own regimen that's right for you. If you listen to your body and start slowly, you'll be reaping the benefits of a sweat bath in no time.

◄ Adjacent to a bathroom shower is the ideal location for a sauna. This allows bathers to easily rinse off after a sauna session. Plus, it eliminates the need to don a robe for the trek from the sauna to the shower.

TALK THE TALK

If you're going to bathe like the Finns, you might as well talk like them. The Finns have a sauna vocabulary that is difficult — and sometimes impossible — to translate. For a quick lesson in Finnish sauna lexicon, check out these words to the wise. Then go forth and impress your friends and family.

But first, some tips on pronunciation. The following is not meant to serve as a complete pronunciation guide, but it will help to explain the lovely lilting sound of the Finnish language.

Each character is always pronounced the same way. That means words are pronounced the way they look and are spelled the way they sound.

Dotted vowels are also pronounced the same way wherever they appear. A dotted *ä* sounds like the *a* in *hat,* and the dotted *ö* sounds like the German *ö* or the French *eu.* A close proximity in English is the *u* in *fur.*

Single characters are pronounced quickly and double ones are drawn out a bit. Think about the difference between the words *boot* and *hut.*

The stress is on the first syllable.

Except for the rules above, the pronunciation is close to Spanish or Italian, with softer consonants.

avanto. A hole in the ice of a frozen lake or sea.

avantouinti. "Ice hole swimming" is the loose translation. It means swimming in a frozen lake or sea. Swimmers cut a large opening through the ice *(avanto)* and either take a quick plunge or swim for a few minutes. It might sound crazy, but *avanto* swimmers maintain that it restores their vigor and makes them feel refreshed.

kippo, kauha. Ladle used to throw water on the hot rocks.

kiuas. A sauna stove or heater. It has rocks *(kiuaskivet)* on top for increased heat production. Humidity is increased in the sauna by throwing water on the hot rocks.

kiulu. Small pail or bucket to contain the *löyly* water. It is usually made of wooden boards secured together with wooden hoops.

lakeinen. The opening in the ceiling of a smoke sauna through which the smoke escapes during heating.

lauteet. The elevated platform or benches in the sauna. Heat rises, so this is the place to relax when

(continued on next page)

you are seeking the hottest temperatures. A single bench is called *laude*.

löyly. Steam or vapor created by throwing water on the heated stones. *Löyly* refers to the resulting steam or to the overall heat, humidity, and temperature in the sauna. *Heittää löylyä* is the action of throwing water on the stones. The hot steam raises the sauna temperature temporarily, and bathers on the top bench might find themselves ducking to avoid the *löyly* near the ceiling. *Löylyhuone* means "the hot room."

pesuhuone. The washing room.

pukuhuone. The dressing room.

räppänä. Duct or vent on the sauna wall close to the ceiling. The size of the opening is often adjustable to allow more or less ventilation.

sauna. A Finnish-style sweat bath or the room where the bath occurs. The correct pronunciation is sow-na (as in "cow"), not saw-na. Related words include *saunoa* (the act of bathing in a sauna) and *saunoja* (a person bathing in a sauna).

savusauna. A smoke sauna, which is the original form of sauna, with no chimney. While the room is being heated, the smoke from the burning wood under the stove fills the sauna and escapes through a hole in the ceiling *(lakeinen)* and through the door, which is usually kept slightly open during heating.

tiku, kisu, kitku. Unpleasant fumes in a smoke sauna right after heating. The fumes dissipate in an hour or two, after which time the sauna is ready. Thanks to electric heaters, *tiku* is no longer an inevitable nuisance for sauna users.

vihta, vasta. A thick bunch of birch twigs about 16 inches (40 cm) in length, which is used to swat oneself to promote blood circulation and cleanse the skin. The twig whisk is not supposed to hurt; rather, it's intended to make the skin tingle for a while. The vihta is made from young twigs with many leaves, making the flagellation soft and pleasant. *Vihtoa* is the action of using the *vihta.*

SAUNA MAINTENANCE

Saunas are one of the easiest home luxury items to maintain. Unlike spas — which have pumps, motors, filters, and heaters — saunas have only heaters to worry about. And unlike spa water, which needs routine monitoring and chemical treatment, a sauna's interior is relatively simple to keep in tip-top shape.

Preventing Problems

Caring for your sauna room will be much easier if you take some preventive steps. First, the floor beneath the duckboards should be properly sealed. This includes concrete floors and the grout lines in ceramic tile floors.

Of course, the less dirt you bring into the sauna, the cleaner it will be. Use a mat in front of the sauna door to wipe feet on. Also, before entering the sauna, bathers should shower to remove excessive dirt, body lotions, hair products, deodorants, and makeup, all of which will drip onto the benches and floor as bathers perspire.

If your sauna is next to a swimming pool, have bathers rinse off after using the pool and before entering the sauna. Otherwise, the chemically treated pool water could discolor the sauna wood.

Insist that bathers place an absorbent terry-cloth towel on the benches before sitting down or reclining. This will prevent most of the perspiration from reaching the bench, while also providing a more comfortable surface on which to relax.

When you are finished using the sauna, it's important to prop the door open to allow air to flow into the room, which will freshen the air and help dry out the interior. You can close the door once the sauna is completely dry and smells clean.

▶ As master baths get larger to accommodate today's spa amenities, saunas are at the top of more and more homeowners' lists of must-haves.

Common Sauna Problems

A well-crafted sauna will give you years of trouble-free use. Solid wall construction, proper insulation, a durable vapor barrier, and quality carpentry will help your sauna last a lifetime. Proper care and maintenance, discussed on page 99, will also ward off problems before they occur.

Assuming you have a well-built sauna, any problems you encounter are probably going to be related to the heater, controls, or electrical system. The following table presents some problems and solutions, but if the situation gets dire, you'll probably need to call in a licensed electrician.

PROBLEM	CAUSE	SOLUTION
There is no power.	Cords are unplugged.	Check the connections to make sure they are secure.
	Circuit breaker has tripped.	Check the breaker box and flip the switch if needed.
The breaker or fuse box is tripping.	Amperage is wrong.	Make sure that the amperage for the breaker is the same as the amperage for the sauna.
	The circuit is overloaded.	Make sure that the circuit is not overloaded. The sauna should have its own circuit with nothing else connected to it.
The heater isn't working.	Overload switch is tripped.	Press the reset button for the overload switch. The owner's manual for your heater will indicate where the switch is located.
	Thermostat is set too low.	Adjust the thermostat.
	The heating element is burned out, there's a short in the electrical circuit, or the control panel is malfunctioning.	If the heater isn't working or isn't generating the high temperatures it once did, call in a qualified electrician to inspect the unit. Don't attempt to take apart the heater or the electrical box yourself, unless you have the tools and training to make heater repairs.
Rocks are disintegrating.	The rocks are old.	Expect to replace the heater rocks every 5 to 10 years. Periodically remove all stones from the heater and clean the trough. Look for any cracked or broken rocks. Do not allow broken rocks to remain in the trough. Over time, the grit they produce can damage the heater.

PROBLEM	CAUSE	SOLUTION
Rocks are dirty.	Something other than clean water was spilled on them.	Clean the rocks after they have completely cooled. Soak them in a soapy (light detergent) mixture of warm water. Wash them off with a sponge, then rinse them in clean water and allow them to dry before placing them back in the heater. Meanwhile, clean the heater of the foreign substance. Gradually build heat in the sauna to totally dry the rocks.
Light is not working.	The bulb is burned out.	Disconnect the main power supply from the sauna and change the lightbulb.
	If the light is connected to the control panel, it may have been manually turned off.	Press the "lamp" button on the control panel to turn the light back on.
The wood is discolored.	The sauna has darkened with age.	This is a natural process of the wood. You can restore the clarity of the wood with a solution of water and oxalic acid. Oxalic acid is used to bleach bare or uncoated wood only. Caution: *Oxalic acid is poisonous. Wear rubber gloves and safety goggles to prevent the chemical from touching your skin or eyes. Also, don't use a metal bucket, which can react with the chemicals.* Before using oxalic acid, read all of the information on the container so you understand the safety precautions and instructions. Before applying the oxalic acid solution, it's important to clean the wood to remove any dirt and grime. You should also test the solution in an inconspicuous spot. You may need to dilute the solution to achieve the desired results or apply it multiple times to remove difficult stains. To lighten and restore the natural tones of the wood without affecting the patina, use 3 to 5 ounces (8 to 15 ml) of oxalic acid per each gallon (3.8 L) of hot water. The solution can be applied with a spray bottle, brush, or cloth. Rinse thoroughly with clean water.
	The wood is stained.	Dissolve 12 to 16 ounces (35 to 47 ml) of oxalic acid crystals in 1 gallon (3.8 L) of hot water. For best results, use the solution while it's hot. With a scrub brush, apply the solution liberally to the wood and allow it to remain until the desired lightness has been achieved. Triple-rinse the wood with clean water and allow it to dry thoroughly. When completely dry, lightly sand the surface, if needed, and wipe it down with a damp cloth.

Routine Care

Once in a while, your sauna needs some special care. Here's a look at the mild nuisances you are likely to encounter at one time or another.

Dirty Floors. Sweep or vacuum the sauna interior periodically to remove dirt, hair, and other debris. Depending on how many bathers use the sauna, the floor may need to be washed regularly to maintain cleanliness. If the floor beneath the duckboards is concrete or ceramic tile, remove the duckboards, wet-mop the floor with a mild cleaning solution, and rinse well. Wipe down the duckboards with a mild surface cleaner and water and replace them after the floor has completely dried. The duckboards may be lightly sanded as needed to remove stubborn soil and stains.

Wet Floors. Use only one or two ladles full of water over the hot rocks at a time. Otherwise, the excess water will cool the rocks and drip to the floor. If too much water has been used you will need to mop up puddles or lift duckboards to enable the floor beneath to dry.

Dirty Benches and Walls. The benches and walls can be washed with a mild soap or detergent dissolved in water. This should be adequate for removing most dirt and perspiration stains. Do not use harsh cleansers or ammonia, which can damage the wood and turn it gray. When cleaning, pay extra attention to areas people touch frequently: benches, doors, and controls. Finally, rinse away any soap residue with a damp cloth and clean water; however, avoid using too much water, which can darken the wood. Never hose down the interior of the sauna.

◀ This prefabricated sauna house includes a spacious sauna, a shower, a dressing room, and a porch for cooling down between sessions. A nearby pool allows bathers to plunge into refreshing water, in much the same way early sauna users jumped into a nearby lake or pond to cool off.

Uneven Doors. Over time some swelling or shrinkage of the door may occur, especially in cold winter climates where there's a dramatic change in humidity from season to season. Depending on the style of door, you might be able to make some adjustments to ensure a better fit. You can refer to your sauna's owner's manual for instructions on how to do this.

Dented or Scratched Wood. Depending on how deep the dent or scratch is, you might be able to remove it with a light sanding using fine-grit sandpaper.

Burned-Out Lights. Traditional lightbulbs tend to burn out faster in the sauna environment than in the rest of the home. When it's time to replace the bulb, choose one that is rated for the same wattage as the fixture. A rough service bulb, like the kind used in automobiles, will last longer. For a cozier sauna environment, use amber-colored lightbulbs, which produce a softer glow.

Grimy Heater. Over time the heater can become dirty or speckled with water spots. If the heater has a stainless-steel casing, you can clean it with a mild, nonabrasive cleaner or a special stainless-steel cleaner. Never use steel wool or scouring pads to clean the metal; these will scratch the surface and leave behind iron specks that will create rust stains.

Soiled Rocks. If anything other than clean water and sauna fragrances is spilled over the rocks, you'll need to clean them. Allow the rocks to cool completely, then soak them in a mild detergent solution, using a sponge or rag to clean them. Rinse them thoroughly and allow them to dry before placing them back in the heater. Also, clean the heater of any foreign substance prior to placing the rocks inside. Finally, gradually build heat in the sauna to totally dry out the rocks.

▲ A conventional sauna heater allows you to ladle (or throw) small amounts of water over the rocks to create a burst of steam. The rise in humidity makes the sauna feel hotter — an experience the Finnish call *löyly*.

Stagnant Water in Buckets. Never allow water to stand in the bucket for more than a day. When it's not in use, empty and clean the bucket before storing it. If you are using a metal bucket instead of a wooden one, don't set it on the top bench, because the high temperatures there could make the bucket too hot to handle.

Good housekeeping will help you maintain your sauna's pristine condition, especially when combined with the diligent use of clean towels on the benches. In fact, with so few components, there is very little that can go wrong, making saunas as easy to care for as your refrigerator. And when was the last time you gave much thought to your icebox?

Steam Baths

5 Getting into Steam Baths

Open any home decorating magazine and you're likely to see a bathroom so beautiful you'll wish you were a towel. You'd be able to hang out there all day.

That's how I feel about my bathroom. Part of the master bedroom suite, it features custom cabinetry, monorail lighting, custom-cast concrete counters, and a spectacular vessel sink made by a local potter. But my favorite amenity is the tiled steam shower, which includes a bench for relaxation, a glass block window to bring in natural light, and a clear glass door to make the space feel larger. Once it fills up with steam, I don't want to leave.

◀ Prefabricated steam rooms take the guesswork out of constructing your own steam bath. Acrylic seats are molded into wall panels, which interlock with an acrylic ceiling to create a watertight room.

My bathroom — even though it occupies a relatively small space — required extensive planning. There were several months of just wishing and longing, followed by a couple more months of serious planning, and concluding with a few more months of actual construction. But it was all time well spent. Indeed, if you plan your steam shower installation with such close attention to details, you'll wish you were a towel, too.

STEAM BATH HISTORY AND CONTEMPORARY TRENDS

Spas, saunas, and steam baths each have a rich history that goes back thousands of years. Oftentimes these histories cross and collide, blurring the lines between warm-water, hot-air, and steam therapies. The terms *sauna* and *steam bath* are frequently used interchangeably, although they have as many differences as similarities. Simply put, a sauna produces a dry heat and a steam bath produces a wet heat. Whereas a sauna might achieve 40 percent humidity through the ladling of water over the hot rocks, a steam bath is able to maintain nearly 100 percent humidity at all times.

Not surprisingly, however, the two types of baths go together like chips and dip. Take ancient Rome, for example, where bathing was a drawn-out affair that involved moving through various baths while socializing with friends and neighbors. Ordinarily, patrons used the *laconicum* (hot-air room) *and* the *caldarium* (steam room), as well as cold-water and hot-water rooms, during their visits.

The use of steam baths originated in Greece and spread westward to Rome. Eventually, the practice migrated north with those Greeks who settled in what is now the Ukraine, part of what was then Russia. The Russians embraced steam baths, or *banya*, for their health and relaxation properties. As

▲ Exquisite tilework evokes the earliest days of the Turkish steam baths. This spacious bath includes multiple showerheads, two drains, and multiple showers, including stationary, handheld, and overhead styles. Tiled alcoves provide a cozy place to bask in the steam.

a result, steam baths are still referred to as Russian baths in many parts of the world.

Throughout history, many cultures have enjoyed steam baths.

Turkish bathhouses, or hammam, were popular in the Middle East and typically included a domed central steam chamber. The Europeans were inspired by the *hammam* when creating their baths. Today "Turkish bath" (like the term "Russian bath") is often used to describe a steam bath.

In India, steam baths, or swedana, are part of the centuries-old Ayurvedic tradition, in which they are used to purify the body as part of the *panchakarma* cleansing process. Wealthy families would often incorporate a *swedana* into their elaborate homes.

Native North Americans constructed steam-infused sweat lodges as part of spiritual rituals. Navajos call theirs *tacheeh,* the process of losing water. The Lakota word is *inikagapi,* which means "to make alive." The more common Lakota word *inipi* is also used, which loosely means "for their life."

In Mexico the Aztecs built beehive-shaped steam baths called **temazcalli.** A fireplace was built outside and shared an adjacent wall with the bath. The raging fire would heat the bath walls. Once inside the small room, bathers would throw water onto the scorching walls to fill the room with steam.

The Finnish sauna tradition also relies on low levels of steam to create **löyly,** which is the wave of hot, moist air that envelops bathers when water is splashed on heated rocks. Some Finns once believed that *löyly* drove out evil spirits.

In Japan one of the first baths was a natural cave in which dry leaves were burned to create heat. The ashes were discarded and straw mats were spread on the ground for bathers. Seawater was then sprinkled on the cave walls to fill the void with steam. Later, in the Edo period, a closet bath was used. This bath was a narrow wooden box containing shallow hot water and a lot of steam. Today the traditional Japanese bath, *ofuro,* is actually a descendant of the Japanese steam baths. And the public baths, *sento,* are still popular.

In Thailand herbal steam baths are a tradition passed down through generations of skilled practitioners in rural temples. Thai herbal medicine incorporates components from various other traditional healing arts, including Indian Ayurvedic remedies, Chinese medicine, and Buddhist traditions. The medicinal steam vapor typically was used to treat skin ailments, muscle stress, and respiratory problems. Another benefit of herbal steam is to prepare the body for a massage. Whatever herbal oil or warming rub the massage therapist applies will be absorbed more readily after the herbal steam, which also makes the muscles more pliable.

◀ An engraving by J. Fumagalli depicts ancient Aztec steam baths. For centuries, steam bathing has been an important tradition for many cultures.

STEAM ROOM VS. SAUNA

While a lot of people enjoy both steam baths and saunas, some people prefer one to the other. Besides the simple fact that steam baths are wet and saunas are dry, here are a few additional points of differentiation:

STEAM ROOM	SAUNA
Steam generator is outside the room.	Sauna heater is inside the room.
Heats water, which is injected into the room as steam.	Heats air, which circulates naturally through intake and outlet vents.
Temperatures rarely exceed 130°F (54°C).	Temperature ranges from 120 to 150°F (49 to 66°C).
Humidity is 100 percent.	Humidity approaches 40 percent.
Walls are constructed of ceramic tile, glass block, acrylic panels, or other nonporous waterproof material.	Walls are constructed of untreated, kiln-dried wood, and they do not have to be waterproof.
Sloped ceiling is highly recommended to divert condensation.	Flat ceiling is recommended to keep heat more evenly dispersed.
Floor drain is required.	Floor drain is not required.

Clearly, steam baths played an important part in hygiene and religious ceremonies in many cultures — especially before the advent of electricity. Today, thanks to technological developments in electric steam generation, it's possible to produce a quick, steady supply of steam and to regulate the temperature within the bath. This has made steam baths viable not only in health clubs and hotels but also in private homes, where they appeal to harried families. After all, who has time to build an *inipi*, stoke a *temazcalli*, or go through the lengthy *panchakarma* ritual?

The first private residential steam baths started to appear in the United States during the 1950s. Since then, the personal steam bath has evolved to include custom-designed and prefabricated steam showers. Aromatherapy oils have long been part of the experience, but advances in steam bath technology have led to these features:

- *Steam generators that eliminate irritating fluctuations in temperature*

- *Softer steam production that doesn't burn bathers*

- *Mood lighting inside the steam shower*

- *Waterproof speakers for listening to CDs or the radio while in the shower*

Though such state-of-the-art amenities certainly add new dimensions to the steam bath experience, the most popular reasons for owning a steam bath are related to health.

The Allure of Steam Baths

The characteristics that draw people to steam baths today are many of the same lures that captivated people centuries ago. Not only is a steam bath enjoyable, but it also contributes to overall health and well-being. Medical science has shown that, like saunas, steam baths are one of the simplest ways to rid the body of toxins and impurities. The hot, moist heat opens pores and encourages millions of sweat glands to perspire. This is significant because sweat contains almost the same elements as urine — which explains why the skin is sometimes referred to as the third kidney. In fact, it is estimated that as much as 30 percent of bodily wastes are eliminated via perspiration.

▲ Steam baths are well known for their health benefits, including detoxification and improved complexion.

Steam baths also encourage muscle relaxation, improve the complexion, promote better sleep, detoxify the body, fight stress, and provide relief for those suffering from upper respiratory problems — everything from asthma to the common cold. Of course, you should always consult your physician before using a steam bath to supplement your health and fitness regimen.

Another benefit of steam bathing is that it stimulates the cardiovascular system. For example, the pulse rate increases from a typical 75 beats per minute to between 100 and 150 beats per minute during a 15- to 20-minute session. Blood pressure, however, remains steady because the tiny blood vessels in the skin expand, accommodating the increased blood flow.

Today some physicians recommend steam baths and saunas for patients who might benefit from self-induced hyperthermia, a condition in which body temperature is higher than normal. Although extreme hyperthermia is dangerous (even deadly), some health experts believe that moderate hyperthermia — 101 to 103°F (38 to 39°C) — is helpful in treating various ailments. The effect is similar to that of a fever, which naturally staves off viruses and bacteria. Hippocrates, the founder of modern medicine, wrote more than two thousand years ago, "Give me the power to create a fever, and I shall cure any disease." Despite this strong endorsement of faux fevers, it's imperative that you never attempt medicinal hyperthermia without proper medical supervision.

Overall, the benefits of steam baths are clear and plentiful. And now that the demand for private steam baths is so high, manufacturers are offering a variety of options to make ownership a reality for anyone. Whether you're building a custom steam

◀ A steam bath can go wherever you have a floor drain. Prefabricated units like this one are easy to install and can fit snugly into tight spaces.

room or installing a prefabricated steam shower, you have many options for creating your perfect steam environment. In many cases you can simply convert an ordinary shower stall or bathtub into a splendid steam area; all you might need is a waterproof ceiling and a watertight door. You can also opt for a prefabricated steam shower, which simplifies the whole design and installation process. Or you can purchase the appropriate steam generator and custom build your steam bath to meet your own floor plan and design aesthetics.

There's no time like the present to warm up to the steam-bath lifestyle. And no matter what type of steam bath you choose, you can rejoice in the fact that you are promulgating a bathing ritual that spans the millennia.

Choosing the Right Steam Bath

Anyone who has ever remodeled or built a home knows all too well that there are countless decisions to be made. He or she may even have the mental scars to prove it. As these courageous homeowners know, just when you think every possible detail has been addressed, you're presented with a dozen more decisions to make. And that's not counting any of the calamities along the way that need to be dealt with.

Selecting the ideal steam bath for you and your family also entails making a fair number of decisions. And the better informed you are about the variety of steam baths out there, the better prepared you'll be to make the tough choices and prevent certain mishaps.

▲ Prefabricated steam showers include everything you need to install the perfect steam bath, from integrated seating and steam doors to watertight ceilings with lighting.

Of course, you've already made the most important decision: to invest in a steam bath. Now let's keep the ball rolling by exploring your options, from the type of steam room you want to the controls that bring it alive.

The Room

Unlike spas and saunas, which can go indoors and outdoors in an array of different locations, the vast majority of steam baths are installed in bathrooms. That's because most residential steam baths double as showers. However, just because the location of your steam bath may be limited doesn't mean your hands are tied when it comes to choosing a steam bath that appeals to your design aesthetic. Of course, you'll have the most design freedom if you incorporate a steam bath when the bathroom is first built or when it is being remodeled. But don't lose heart. There are plenty of options for those who simply want to retrofit an existing tub or shower into a luxurious steam bath.

Whatever type of steam bath you decide on, it must be watertight to protect the surrounding area from moisture damage. Here's a brief look at the major choices you have.

CUSTOM STEAM BATHS

Custom steam baths give you the most design flexibility. Working with an interior or bathroom designer, you can create a steam bath that perfectly fits the space available and that is built from materials that complement the rest of the home. Though tile is the most popular surface for custom steam baths, you may also use stone, glass blocks, glass panels, acrylic, or other nonporous materials. And because of the custom nature, these steam baths don't have to be in the bathroom, nor do they have to include a shower. As long as you have a waterproof room with a floor drain, you have tremendous design freedom.

PREFABRICATED STEAM BATHS

Similar to prefabricated spas and saunas, prefabricated steam baths take much of the hassle out of installation. After preparing the floor and drain, you simply assemble the unit, including the walls and ceiling. These kits come with all of the necessary hardware, as well as silicone for ensuring watertight seals. Like a custom steam bath, these units can be installed almost anywhere you have a waterproof floor and proper drainage, and they don't have to include a shower.

RETROFITTED STEAM BATHS

If you don't have the room or desire to install a separate steam bath in your home, you can opt to retrofit an existing tub or shower stall so that it can double as a steam bath. These systems typically include a waterproof ceiling unit that caps the tub or shower and a special door that ensures a watertight enclosure. You'll need to make sure that you have proper access to water lines and a power source in order to hook up the steam generator.

The Steam Generator

The main purpose of a steam bath is to envelop you in steam so that you can detoxify your body through sweat. Without a steam generator, there is no steam bath, which is why you must take measures to ensure that you're getting the right one for your unique situation.

A steam generator, when activated, converts water to steam. It's composed of a water feed and leveling system, a stainless-steel water reservoir, and an industrial-grade heating element. About the size of a briefcase, the steam generator automatically takes in water, boils it, and delivers hot steam to the chamber.

A steam generator is classified by the power rating of its heating elements, measured in kilowatts. The higher the kilowatts, the faster it's able to produce steam. Though the smallest steam generators may be able to run on 120 volts, most units need to be connected to a 240-volt line. A licensed electrician should do this installation; otherwise, the warranty may become void.

When properly sized, the steam generator should be able to produce a bath temperature of 115 to 125°F (46 to 52°C) with 98 percent humidity. The correct size is typically determined by finding the cubic space of the steam room (length × width × height); however, other factors influence sizing, such as steam bath design and construction materials. For more information on sizing steam

STEAM GENERATOR

With every steam generator, fresh hot or cold water is heated to produce steam, which is forced through copper tubing connected to the steam head. The generator shuts off after a set time or when the desired temperature is reached, whichever happens first.

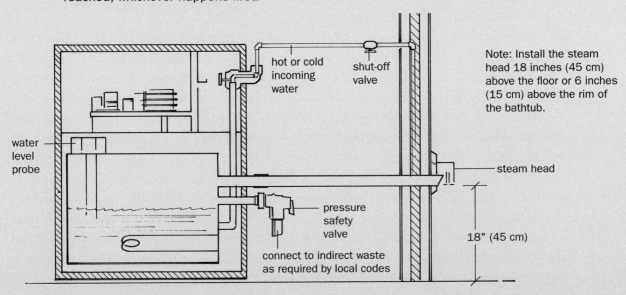

Note: Install the steam head 18 inches (45 cm) above the floor or 6 inches (15 cm) above the rim of the bathtub.

water level probe

hot or cold incoming water

shut-off valve

steam head

pressure safety valve

18" (45 cm)

connect to indirect waste as required by local codes

▲ Custom steam doors can fit any opening with the addition of side panels and transoms above the door. Some however, are made in limited sizes, so they work best with new construction.

generators, see Sizing a Steam Generator on page 122.

It's important to note that not all steam generators are created equal. Some produce a softer steam that is less likely to burn bathers as it is being emitted. Ideally, you should shop around and experience different steam systems to find the one you like best. However, note that you can purchase a steam deflector shield to create a more pleasurable bathing environment. When placed over the steam head, the deflector disperses the steam flow, thereby reducing "hot spots" and creating a more comfortable experience.

Some steam generators operate more quietly than others. You might want to find ways to muffle your generator's noise.

Some units have an automatic draining system that ensures fresh water is used for each steam bath. This also prevents stagnant water from standing in the unit, where bacteria can breed and scale can build up.

Finally, most steam heads contain a reservoir for essential oils used in aromatherapy. When the steam comes out of the head, it carries the fragrance throughout the shower. If this is important to you, make sure your steam head has this feature.

The Controls

Controls put the world of steam bathing at your fingertips. Some simply allow you to turn the steam generator on and off, while others permit you to set the maximum temperature of the steam bath, program how long the steam generator will run, and control lights inside the chamber.

Control panels are typically mounted on the wall outside the steam bath, but ancillary watertight controls can be installed inside the bath for convenience. Most manufacturers offer control panels in a variety of finishes — from white and black to brushed nickel and gold — so you can match them to the rest of your decor. Some steam generator manufacturers are using radio-frequency technology to make remote controls that can be used inside or outside the steam bath.

The Door

An important factor in creating a watertight steam bath is installing a door fitted with a full gasket and rated for steam bath use. Unless the door seals off the steam bath completely, moisture will escape and cause damage to the surrounding area.

Prefabricated steam baths include a door, as do most retrofit systems. Custom steam baths, however, typically require custom-fit doors. After the bath is completely built, precise measurements are taken of the bottom, top, and both sides of the door opening to ensure a perfect fit.

Doors come in a variety of configurations, including sliding and swing designs. If necessary, they can incorporate side and top glass panels to accommodate almost any opening. Top panels may be hinged so they can promote air circulation during regular showers and after use, when you want the steam bath to dry out. Door frames can be ordered in a variety of finishes to complement any decor.

The Benches

For maximum comfort, you'll probably want to incorporate seating in your steam bath. The typical steam bath lasts 15 to 20 minutes, which is a long time to be standing idle.

Custom steam baths afford several bench options:

Integrated Bench. A bench that is framed in as part of the bath enclosure and surfaced with the same waterproof material used elsewhere in the steam bath.

Cantilevered Bench. A bench, mounted on specially designed metal supports, that juts from the wall and is open underneath. The supports mount to wall studs and can be surfaced with the same waterproof material used elsewhere in the steam bath.

Prefabricated Bench. These units mount to the wall and have a flip-down seat. They can be made of acrylic or wood.

Wooden Bench. Somewhat like the benches in a sauna, these built-in or stand-alone benches are made of kinds of woods that can weather the extreme moisture and heat of a steam bath.

Retrofitted steam baths will probably use a prefabricated bench or a wooden bench, whereas prefabricated steam baths will typically include acrylic benches molded into the wall panels of the bath.

HAVE A SEAT

Options abound when it comes to choosing a seat for your steam bath. You may opt to build a custom-tiled bench, but if you are retrofitting an existing tub or shower, a flip-up, wall-mounted seat, or even a freestanding bench may be necessary.

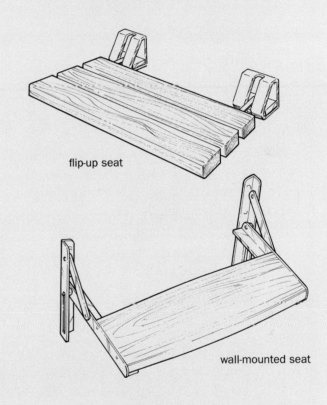

flip-up seat

wall-mounted seat

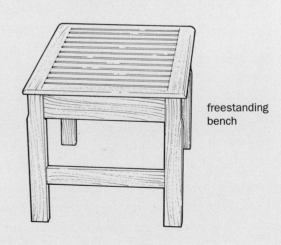

freestanding bench

Other Amenities

As if the luxurious sensation of soothing steam isn't enough, manufacturers offer a range of accessories to make the steam bath even more marvelous. When deciding what type of steam bath environment you're trying to create, consider the following:

- *Fog-free mirrors*
- *Vapor-proof lighting*
- *Colored mood lighting*
- *Waterproof speakers*
- *Aromatherapy essential oils*
- *Waterproof remote controls*

Clearly, the benefits of steam bathing can be realized by anyone willing to invest in it—whether you intend to build an elaborate customized bath or merely retrofit a fiberglass shower stall. Whatever your intentions, the following section details the planning and design process.

▲ Though the bathtub takes center stage in this installation, the steam bath makes a wonderful backdrop. Two doors provide easy access, and dual steam heads ensure that the space is heated quickly.

DESIGNING THE STEAM BATH ENVIRONMENT

One of the wonderful things about steam baths is that they can be as simple or as sophisticated as you want. You can easily convert an existing bathtub into a steam bath, or you can build an elaborate steam room from scratch using a custom design or a prefabricated unit. Either way, you can't go wrong, because steam is steam, and you can realize its benefits whether you spend one thousand dollars to retrofit a small shower or ten thousand dollars to outfit an elaborate custom steam bath.

Regardless of your budget, however, you won't be able to bask in the soothing mist of your personal steam bath until you've made some preliminary decisions. With careful planning, you can rest assured that the final result will be the perfect marriage of design and function. To get you started, here are some key questions that will help you better understand the type of steam bath you want.

What type of steam bath appeals to you? The previous section briefly outlined the differences among custom, prefabricated, and retrofitted steam baths. One of them is bound to suit your situation better than the others.

How big will your steam bath be? As with saunas, you'll want to keep the steam bath as small as possible to ensure efficient heating. At the same time, you want it to be large enough for you to move around, sit, and possibly recline. Steam rises, so you don't want the steam bath any taller than is necessary. In most cases, 7 feet (2.1 m), which enables most people to stand comfortably inside, is high enough. If you want your steam bath taller, you'll need to size your steam generator accordingly to ensure you have sufficient steam where bathers sit.

STEAM BATH SELECTION

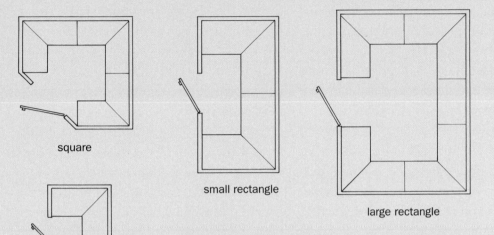

square

small rectangle

large rectangle

cut-corner

Prefabricated, modular steam baths come in a variety of sizes to accommodate two or more bathers. Square, rectangular, and cut-corner designs are available to provide more design options.

What shape will it be? Though most steam baths are square or rectangular, some units have cut corners or curves, which allow them to fit better in tight quarters. Prefabricated and retrofit units offer little flexibility here, but the sky's the limit when it comes to custom installations. The one thing all steam baths have in common, however, is a sloped ceiling. To prevent condensation from dripping on bathers, the ceiling should be sloped at least 2 inches (5 cm) for every foot (30 cm) of distance. If you want to maximize the height in your steam bath, consider sloping the ceiling from the center.

Where will you install the steam bath? Most steam baths are incorporated into a bathroom, but you can build them anywhere you have a waterproof floor that slopes to a drain and access to water and electrical services. If you want a steam bath that can be enjoyed by more than two or three people, you might want to install it in a home gym, adjacent to an indoor pool or spa, or beside a sauna.

Will you have any adjacent facilities? If you have room next to the steam bath, consider adding amenities that complement the home health spa lifestyle, such as a sauna, a spa, a changing room, and lounge chairs for cooling down. If your steam bath doesn't include a shower, you should have one nearby for use after the steam bath.

What materials will you use for the walls and ceiling? If you are using a prefabricated steam bath or converting an acrylic tub or shower into a steam bath with a retrofit system, this decision has been made for you by the manufacturer. With a custom steam bath, however, you can choose tile, natural stone, glass panes or blocks, acrylic panels, or other nonporous surfaces for the walls. Wherever possible, you should insulate the walls to prevent heat loss, especially if any of the walls are on the exterior of the home, where heat loss is the greatest.

Depending on the type of materials you use, the walls may need some preliminary work before the steam bath is installed. For example, tiled walls require a backing of concrete board, which is more impervious to water than regular drywall. This is typically installed by your tiler, who would also create the floor (or shower pan) for your steam bath. Glass block and stacked stone, in contrast, will require a foundation that can support their weight. Your mason will be able to guide you in this process.

If your steam bath contains a window, it must have double panes and a nonporous frame that is completely sealed. Skylights must be sealed off at the ceiling height with a glass pane, clear acrylic sheet, or some other transparent material.

▲ Large and tall steam baths may require multiple steam heads to effectively heat the bath.

What type of floor surface will you use? The most common floor surfaces are tile and stone. It's imperative that the floor slopes toward the drain so that there is no standing water and that water doesn't pool near the walls. This is not a concern if you are retrofitting an existing bath or shower unit, but it is an issue with custom construction. In most cases you will need a tile setter to create a "shower pan" from mortar that slopes toward the drain. The pan can be surfaced with tile or natural stone to match the rest of the steam bath. However, it's important for the tile professional to install a rubber membrane beneath the pan in case it cracks. This will ensure that water still runs to the drain and won't damage the floor beneath.

What type of door will you use? Prefabricated steam baths typically come with a door specified by the manufacturer. If you are retrofitting a bathtub, you'll most likely use a watertight sliding door, similar to regular sliding bathtub doors. For small shower stalls, you'll use a swinging glass door. Depending on the width and height of your steam bath, you may need to incorporate glass panels on the top and sides of the door.

Custom steam baths, once again, give you the greatest design freedom. You can specify doors with or without side and top panels. And the top panes can be hinged to allow air to circulate, which is useful for drying out the steam bath or ventilating it during a shower.

Doors should be about 36 inches (0.9 m) wide to allow easy access but no taller than 84 inches (2.1 m). Openings larger than that require side and top panels because the hinges cannot support the weight of the door. Also, plan whether you want the door to swing to the left or to the right.

To ensure a perfect fit, the door for a custom steam bath should be specially made.

SCORES OF DOORS

Standard steam doors come in a variety of styles to match your typical prefabricated shower or bath stall. However, custom doors in a variety of configurations can accommodate most any design you conceive.

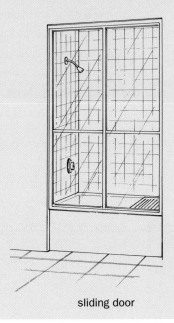

sliding door

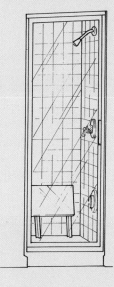

single-pane door

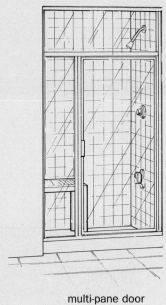

multi-pane door

This entails taking precise measurements of the door opening, including the top width, bottom width, left height, and right height. This allows the manufacturer to accommodate openings that aren't perfectly square.

When placing your order, you can also specify the frame finish and type of glass you want. Finishes are typically available in silver, gold, brushed nickel, satin nickel, white, almond, and bronze. Glass panels are available in clear, etched, frosted, and patterned designs, enabling you to create a totally transparent steam bath or one that completely obscures bathers.

What type of lighting will you use? If you have a lot of natural light flooding into your steam bath, you should still include a light for nighttime use. The light should be vapor-proof and rated for steam bath use. You should also determine whether you want the light operated by a separate switch or by the steam bath control panel. If you want it hooked up to the control panel, make sure you purchase a control panel that includes a light function. Otherwise, you can purchase lights that operate with remote controls. Some even have colored bulbs that enable you to create a mood with yellow, red, and blue lights.

What kind of seats will you have and where will they go? Depending on the design of your steam bath, you may be restricted to wall-mounted seats that flip up when not in use or molded seats that are part of acrylic wall panels. For retrofitted steam baths and showers, you can also purchase portable shower seats that are easily removed when not in use.

Not surprisingly, custom steam baths leave you with plenty of seating options, from built-in tiled ledges to wooden benches. When placing benches, be careful not to position them too close to the steam head or where they might hinder bathers from getting in and out of the steam bath. Make sure that the seats slope slightly toward the center of the steam bath so that water is able to drain freely.

What size of steam generator will you use? Steam generators must be correctly sized or you risk having a disappointing steam bath experience. Manufacturers rate their steam generators by kilowatts and specify how much space each generator can accommodate. However, many factors can affect the performance of a steam unit, from the materials used in constructing the stall to the ambient air temperature outside the stall.

▲ Expansive panes of glass enable this contemporary steam bath to be one with nature.

For more information on selecting the right steam generator, see Sizing a Steam Generator on page 122.

Be aware that some steam generators produce softer steam and operate more quietly than others, so shop around and test a few if possible. In addition, if you're interested in aromatherapy, look for a steam generator that includes a reservoir for essential oils.

Where will the steam generator be installed? A steam generator can be placed inside a bathroom cabinet, installed inside a waterproof, enclosed bench within a custom steam bath, or remotely located elsewhere in the home, such as in the basement or utility closet. Wherever you decide to place your steam generator, make sure you have the following items for proper installation:

- *Electrical line from the main panel to the steam generator (120 or 240 volts, depending on the generator)*

- *Water line from a source (preferably hot) to the steam generator, terminating with a shut-off valve and appropriate backflow device*

- *Copper steam line running from steam generator to where the steam head will be positioned*

- *Pressure-relief valve line plumbed to a drainage pipe*

- *Drain pan plumbed to a discharge*

- *Drain valve plumbed to a discharge*

- *Control wiring run from steam generator to the location of the control panel*

For best performance, the steam generator shouldn't be located more than 25 feet (7.6 m) from the steam head. It also should be easily accessible for repairs and maintenance. The manufacturer's installation manual will detail specific guidelines to follow, but you may also want to check local building codes to make sure your installation meets their restrictions. Never install the steam generator freestanding inside the steam bath, outdoors, or where it may be subjected to freezing conditions.

The steam line should never form a gully where water could stand and foster bacteria. The line should always be angled toward the steam generator or (last resort) the steam head. Any steam line longer than 10 feet (3 m) should be insulated to prevent steam from condensing before it reaches the bath.

By answering these key questions, you'll be better prepared to design the perfect steam bath for your home and your family. Shelter magazines, bathroom design books, and bathroom designer showrooms will give you some additional ideas for creating the look you want. Unlike with a spa or sauna, you probably won't be able to test your steam bath before purchase, especially if it's a custom installation. Doing your homework during the planning stage will help ensure that your steam bath looks and performs the way you want it to.

PLACE OF ITS OWN

A steam generator can be placed in a vanity, a basement, or a nearby closet (three possibilities shown below). The primary requirement is that it be level, accessible, and, most desirably, 25 feet (7.6 m), but not more than 50 feet (15.2 m) away from the steam room. Also, the steam tubing must not have any dips in it that could prevent water from draining either to the steam head or back to the generator.

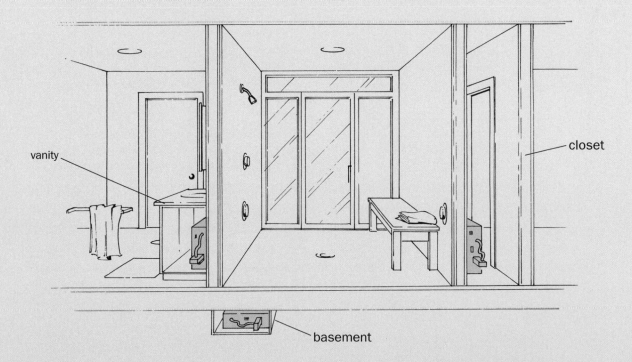

vanity

closet

basement

SIZING A STEAM GENERATOR

A properly sized steam generator should enable your steam bath to reach the desired temperature in 10 to 20 minutes. An undersized generator will take longer and may never achieve the temperatures you want. If the unit is oversized, there might be an unbearably hot area around the steam head.

A steam generator uses a heating element to produce steam. The amount of steam that the unit is able to produce is determined by the kilowatt rating of the generator. The more kilowatts, the easier time the unit will have creating heat. Understandably, a large steam bath requires a more powerful steam generator than a small one does.

Certain construction materials and steam bath designs also have a negative impact on the effectiveness of steam generators. Therefore, the following must be taken into account:

• *Ceiling heights greater than 7 feet (2.1 m)*

• *Building materials that conduct heat and are poor insulators, such as glass blocks and tile*

• *Ambient room temperatures that are lower than 68 to 72°F (20 to 22°C)*

• *Wall temperatures (exterior walls in cold climates require additional heating power)*

• *Surface area (most steam generator sizing charts assume a rectangular room, but irregular-shaped rooms may create more surface area and require additional heating power)*

There is no single precise way to accommodate for all of these factors when sizing a steam generator, but some formulas will help you narrow down your selection.

The first thing you'll need to do is figure out the cubic footage of the steam bath enclosure. This is simply a matter of multiplying the length times the width times the height. Do not deduct for built-in benches, because these have a surface area equal to that of the space without a bench, and it is the surface area that affects heat loss.

Manufacturers publish charts indicating how many cubic feet can be heated by the various generators they offer. This chart gives you some idea of how steam generators are sized.

MAXIMUM CUBIC FEET	KILOWATTS
100	4.5
200	6.5
300	8.0
400	10.0
500	12.0
650	14.0

Next, factor in the construction materials used. The Steamist Company, a manufacturer of steam generators, offers this formula: Take the overall cubic foot measurement and adjust that number for the construction material you're using (see the list at top right). If you're using more than one type of construction material, select the one with the greatest heat loss.

CONSTRUCTION MATERIAL	MULTIPICATION FACTOR
Fiberglass, acrylic, or cultured marble	.008
Ceramic tile on cement board	1.25
Ceramic tile on mortar bed	1.30
Glass or glass block	1.35
Porcelain tile on cement board	1.60
Natural stone tile such as marble, travertine, slate, or granite (1/8 to 1/2 inch thick) on cement board	1.90
Natural stone tile (3/8 to 1/2 inch thick) on mortar board	2.00
Natural stone tile on stone slab	2.25

- Add 10% for each insulated exterior wall.

- Select the next larger steam generator if the steam bath includes a skylight or window.

- If the adjusted steam bath requirement falls between the capacity of two models of steam generators, always choose the one that's rated higher.

EXAMPLE: A steam bath that measures 4 x 6 x 8 feet and is built out of ceramic tile on cement board, with two exterior walls.

Capacity = 4 x 6 x 8 = 192 cubic feet

Multiply by 1.25 for tile on cement board
= 240 cubic feet

Add 20% for two exterior walls
= 288 cubic feet

MrSteam, another steam generator manufacturer, has a different formula for sizing steam generators. The company suggests taking your overall cubic foot measurement and increasing it by the following percentages if they apply to your steam bath:

- Each exterior outside wall or uninsulated crawl space   15%

- Tile on mud mortar walls   15%

- Extra glass panel in addition to the door   15%

- Cast-iron tub or marble bench   15%

- Each foot after exceeding 8 feet (2.4 m) in height   15%

- Interior walls that are marble, stone, shale, granite, glass block, or concrete   100%

EXAMPLE: A steam bath that measures 4 x 6 x 8 feet and is built out of ceramic tile on cement board, with two exterior walls.

Capacity = 4 x 6 x 8 = 192 cubic feet

Plus 15% for tile on cement board
= 220.8 cubic feet

Plus 30% for two exterior walls
= 287.4 cubic feet

The results of these two formulas are roughly the same, and both would point you to a similarly sized steam generator — in this case, one that is rated at 8 to 9 kilowatts.

6 Getting the Most out of Steam Baths

I see my life as a series of moments, each of which can be lived to its fullest or frittered away. (I'll admit, some days frittering is the fullest way to live life.) That's why I strive to get the most out of every moment. "Multitasking" is my mantra. For example, I've found that if I turn on my steam shower first thing in the morning, it's ready to go by the time I've brushed my teeth and fired up Mr. Coffee. During the long Wisconsin winters, there's no better way to begin the day than with a hot shower, a hot steam bath, and a hot cup of joe.

◀ This unique steam bath (designed by Rebecca Swanston of Swanston & Associates) has a natural stone wall that contains the steam head and hides the floor drain. Glass surrounds the other three sides, and the entire shower is capped with safety glass. Wooden benches accommodate several bathers and are long enough for lounging. A towel warmer on the wall outside the steam bath adds another luxurious amenity.

I enjoy steam baths the rest of the year, too. Taken an hour before bedtime, a steam bath promotes a deep and restful sleep. After a workout, it relaxes my tired and sore muscles. During a cold, it promotes freer breathing. Combined with aromatherapy, it lifts my spirits and clears my mind. These are just a few of the steam shower instances that pepper my life. And if you make the most of your misty shower moments, you'll quickly discover that time spent basking in the steam is one of the best ways to spend the moments of your life.

STEAM BATH ENJOYMENT AND SAFETY

A wonderful thing about owning a steam bath is that it's so easy and convenient to enjoy. Unlike a sauna, which may take 30 to 45 minutes to heat up, a steam bath will reach a desired temperature in just 10 minutes or so, which allows it to fit effortlessly into even the most hectic daily schedule. If you're already planning to take a shower, a steam bath doesn't add many more minutes to your morning regimen. Likewise, a quick steam bath before going to bed will more than make up for the time by rewarding you with a deeper, more restful sleep.

The health benefits of steam bathing are well known. Like a sauna, a steam bath is able to hyperthermia, whereby the internal temperature of the body is elevated above normal. If the environmental temperature exceeds that of the body, it isn't able to cool down, no matter how profusely it sweats. In other words, the body cannot maintain a normal temperature when the environmental temperature is as high as that generated by a steam bath. Thus, the body temperature rises above normal. As the body sweats in its attempt to cool down, toxins are flushed out. This stimulates

▲ Steam doors come in a lot of styles and configurations, from hinged models to sliding versions like the one shown here. This makes it possible to retrofit many existing bathtubs and showers into steam baths.

the immune system and slows down the growth of bacteria and viruses. Meanwhile, the production of white blood cells, the primary agents of the immune system, increases. The creation of antibodies also speeds up.

The rise in body temperature depends largely on three factors: the temperature and humidity of the steam bath, the bather's propensity to sweat, and the time spent in the steam bath. Depending on the temperature and duration, a steam bath is capable of producing the same thermal effects on the body

STEAM BATH SAFETY

Before entering the steam room, keep in mind a few precautions:

● *Heat increases your body's cardiovascular activity.* Unless you have no health problems, consult a physician before using a steam bath. He or she may recommend that you avoid steam bathing if you have high blood pressure, heart disease, or other cardiovascular problems.

● *Steam bathing is not recommended for pregnant women, small children, or the elderly.*

● *Do not use a steam bath if you have a fever or an open wound,* both of which could worsen in the steam heat.

● *A steam bath is a great way to relax after a workout,* but make sure your body has had time to cool down before subjecting it to the extreme heat of a steam bath.

● *Until you know what your body can handle, limit steam bathing* sessions to 15 to 20 minutes. Do not push yourself beyond what is comfortable. The goal is not to see how long you can withstand the heat but to allow your mind and body to rejuvenate in the relaxing bath.

● *Drink plenty of water before and after the steam bath* to replenish fluids lost during bathing. The possibility of dehydration is not something to take lightly.

● *Do not approach steam bathing as a weight-loss method.* Most of the weight lost in a steam bath consists of fluids. Once they are replenished, the weight will return. Instead, think of steam bathing as a way to relax and detoxify the body.

● *Wait at least one hour after eating a heavy meal before using the steam bath.*

● *Don't use a steam bath while under the influence of alcohol or drugs.*

that a sauna does, even though the steam bath's temperatures are lower. That's because the high levels of humidity in a steam bath off-set the lower temperatures. You've probably heard someone downplay 100-degree days in the Southwest by saying, "It's not that bad; it's a dry heat." Indeed, humidity is a major factor in our perception of temperature. The same 100-degree day in the muggy Midwest would make us much hotter because our sweating bodies wouldn't be able to cool off as efficiently.

Anyone who has suffered from a cold or the flu knows the soothing effects of steam therapy. Steam bathing, and thus steam inhalation, is an effective treatment in respiratory conditions and is highly recommended for the treatment of the common cold, sinusitis, bronchitis, allergies, and asthma.

Among other benefits, steam is credited with relieving discomfort associated with the following:

- *Inflammation and congestion of the upper respiratory membranes*

- *Throat irritation and coughing*

- *Dry mucous membranes*

- *Spasmodic breathing*

- *Clogged mucus in the throat and lungs*

- *Sore muscles*

The enjoyment and benefits afforded by a steam bath depend largely on maintaining the optimum temperature, which falls between 110 and 120°F (43 to 49°C), depending on personal preference. Not only are these temperatures the most pleasant, they also offer the most health benefits. In fact, if the maximum temperature is exceeded by as little as 4 to 6°F (2 to 3°C), the steam bath can be too hot to bear. That's why it's important

▲ Few things compare to the warm embrace of a steam bath.

to have a steam bath control system that reliably regulates the temperature.

How to Take a Steam Bath

There is no single correct way to take a steam bath. But here are some general guidelines. For the most part, they follow the same process used in taking a sauna. Feel free to modify them to fit your own personal preferences.

1. *Turn on the steam generator and set the desired temperature on the control panel.*

2. *Remove clothing and jewelry* while you wait for the steam room to reach a comfortable temperature.

3. *Enter the steam bath and close the door* to prevent steam from escaping. Some people prefer to shower before enjoying a steam bath. If your steam bath includes a shower, you can do so now. Otherwise, use a separate shower to cleanse your body before entering the steam enclosure.

▲ A hinged transom above the steam door is a great way to bring in fresh air and to help dry out the steam shower after each use.

4. *Sit on a bench and relax* as the warm steam releases tension and refreshes your body.

5. *Place a small amount of scented oil in the special reservoir* on the steam head, if it has one, for an aromatherapy experience. You can also spray diluted fragrance directly in the air.

6. *Take a hot shower with the steam for a different sensation if your steam room has a shower.* Note that a cool shower will cause the steam to condense, eliminating the steam bath effect. You may want to bathe with a loofah to scrub your body and promote circulation.

7. *Limit your steam bath to 15 to 20 minutes,* after which you can cool off by taking a shower, dipping into a pool, or simply entering some cool, fresh air. The longer you spend in the steam bath, the longer it will take for you to cool down. Take this time to replenish your fluids.

8. *Some people enjoy two or three sessions in the steam bath.* If you have a hot tub or sauna, you can alternate among them, but be sure to cool down from each bath before entering another one.

9. *Follow up your final steam bath with a warm shower* if you're going to bed or planning to relax. Take a cool shower to awaken the senses and prepare you for the day ahead or an evening on the town.

10. *Refrain from eating for at least one hour before a steam bath* to ensure your body isn't overtaxed. And diligently replace lost liquids with water, nonalcoholic beverages, and fruit and vegetable juices.

STEAM BATH MAINTENANCE

Anyone who has performed domestic chores knows all about tub, tile, and window cleaners. And, if you can clean a bathtub or shower, you can certainly clean a steam bath enclosure. The trickier task is maintaining the steam generator in tip-top condition. But first things first. Let's look at the parts of a steam bath.

The Enclosure

Whether your steam bath is surfaced with tile, acrylic, glass panels, or natural stone, avoid abrasive cleansers that can scratch or dull the surface. Instead, use warm water and liquid detergents specifically designed for your application. When trying out a new cleanser, it's always a good idea to test it in an inconspicuous location before using it on the entire enclosure. Here are some guidelines for using cleansers:

● *Wipe surfaces immediately after applying cleansers.*

● *Don't permit cleansers to sit or dry on the surfaces.*

● *Rinse surfaces completely with water to prevent soap buildup.*

Also, always use a soft cloth — such as an old T-shirt or piece of flannel — to prevent scratches. Even if you're attempting to remove stubborn stains or calcium deposits, never use abrasive materials such as scouring pads, steel wool, scrapers, bristle brushes, sandpaper, or anything else that could scratch or dull the surface. You can use a shower squeegee to clean glass doors.

Oftentimes you can restore the luster of acrylic or fiberglass surfaces with an automotive polishing compound applied with a clean cotton rag. Then rub on a light coat of liquid wax and buff the surface until it shines. Deep scratches may require professional restoration.

Note: When using any cleaning or polishing materials, read and follow all package instructions carefully. Wear rubber gloves at all times and avoid contact with eyes, skin, clothing, rugs, and furnishings. Make sure all cleansers are rinsed off thoroughly.

Wiping down the steam bath after each use is a good habit to get into, especially if you have hard water that leaves water spots and calcium deposits. (If necessary, you can route the water for your steam generator through a water softener to prevent scale buildup.) When cleaning, pay close attention to the corners, where dirt and grime easily accumulate. Also, be sure to disinfect the benches and floor to keep the steam bath sanitized for the next user.

Besides routine cleaning, you should periodically inspect the walls, ceiling, and seat to make sure they're structurally sound.

The Steam Generator

The steam bath generator requires little maintenance. Periodically, inspect the steam generator, steam head, fittings, and plumbing connections for water leaks and malfunctions. Left unchecked, even the smallest leak can cause severe water damage. The control panels should be inspected regularly and cleaned as necessary. Simply use a soft cloth and warm water to gently rub away any water spots or grime. Never use cleansers, abrasives, or detergents on the controls, which can scratch or discolor the faceplate.

◀ Steam bath enclosures typically double as showers, and maintenance isn't any-more difficult than caring for a traditional acrylic or fiberglass shower unit.

MAKING SENSE OF SCENTS

One of the most enjoyable ways to enhance the steam bath is to use essential oils to create an aromatic sanctuary. Aromatherapy is the art and science of using essences from fragrant plants to promote mental and physical health. Essential oils are highly concentrated aromatic extracts that are distilled from a variety of aromatic plants, from grasses, leaves, and flowers to fruit peels, roots, and wood. In a holistic sense, aromatherapy is a preventive approach as well as a proactive approach to treating various ailments. The steam bath offers the perfect environment to experiment and enjoy the various essential oils.

When inhaled, essential oils send messages directly into the limbic system. Here, odors can trigger memories, influencing emotions and behavior. These memories may cause you to relax, to gain a sense of balance, or to be stimulated and uplifted.

While an aroma triggers a response in your brain, the essential oil is drawn into your lungs, supplying physical benefits as well. Aromatherapy works differently on different people, and, in fact, you may react in different ways to the same oils depending on the time of day, your mood, or your surroundings.

French chemist and scholar Rene-Maurice Gattefosse is credited with coining the term *aromatherapie* in 1928, although his interest in essential oils began in 1910. That's when Gattefosse badly burned his hand during an experiment in a perfumery plant. He plunged his hand into the nearest tub of liquid, which happened to be the essential oil from lavender. Later he was amazed at how quickly his burn healed, and with little scarring. This experience started his interest in essential oils and inspired him to experiment with them on wounded soldiers during World War I. He used essential oils from lavender, thyme, lemon, and clove — which have antiseptic properties — and noted that the wounds treated with these oils healed faster, and without some of the disadvantages associated with other antiseptic agents commonly used.

Aromatherapy is not intended to replace traditional medicine or health care, but it is a helpful tool for balancing body, mind, and spirit. About 100 essential oils are used frequently. Following are some of the most popular ones. These can be placed in the special reservoir on the steam head or diluted per the supplier's instructions for spritzing in the steam bath. These oils are highly concentrated and should be used in small amounts. Some may burn the skin if applied directly. Consult an aromatherapy book for more information.

Clary Sage. Bright, earthy, herbaceous, with a subtle fruity note. Natural painkiller. Helpful in treating muscular aches and pains, coughing, exhaustion, sore throat, and stress.

Eucalyptus. Fresh, medicinal, woody, earthy. An antiseptic stimulant good for viral, fungal, and bacterial infection. Effective for respiratory problems such as coughs, colds, and asthma. Also helps to boost the immune system and relieve muscle tension.

Geranium. Floral, fresh, sweet, with a fruity note. Helps to balance hormones in women and is good for balancing the skin. Can be both relaxing and uplifting.

Lavender. Fresh, sweet, floral, herbaceous, slightly fruity. Relaxes and balances both mind and body. Aids sleep, soothes tired muscles, and boosts the immune system. Encourages relaxation and tranquility, has some antiseptic qualities, and is beneficial for the skin.

Lemon. Very uplifting, yet relaxing. Helpful in treating wounds and infections, including colds and flu.

Peppermint. Minty, reminiscent of peppermint candies. More fragrant than spearmint. Useful in treating headaches, muscle aches, and digestive disorders.

Roman Chamomile. Bright, crisp, sweet, fruity, herbaceous. Very relaxing, and can help with sleeplessness and anxiety. Also good for muscle aches and tension. Useful in treating wounds and infection.

Rosemary. Fresh, herbaceous, sweet, slightly medicinal. Very stimulating and uplifting. Is mentally stimulating and boosts the immune system. Treats muscle aches, arthritis, dandruff, dull skin, exhaustion, gout, dry hair, and poor circulation.

Tea Tree. Medicinal, fresh, woody, earthy, herbaceous. Natural antifungal oil, good for treating all sorts of fungal infections. Also helps to boost the immune system.

Ylang Ylang. Fresh, floral, sweet, slightly fruity, yet delicate. Helps one to relax and can reduce muscle tension. Also used to treat anxiety, depression, hypertension, heart palpitations, and stress.

Different users may respond differently to the same essential oils. Also, some essences can have a negative effect on users. While experimentation with essential oils can be fun and beneficial, be sure to check with a physician before making aromatherapy part of any medicinal regimen.

BENEFITS OF ESSENTIAL OILS

According to the National Association for Holistic Aromatherapy (NAHA), essential oils have proven to be effective in treating a wide range of maladies and conditions, as listed below.

Emotional Conditions	*Medical Conditions*	*Skin Conditions*
Anxiety	Bruises, sprains, strains	Acne
Depression	Burns (including sunburn)	Bacterial infections
Fear	Digestive disorders	Cellulite
Grief	Fatigue	Dermatitis
Hopelessness	Fungal infections (such as	Dry skin
Insomnia	athlete's foot and nail fungus)	Eczema
Irritability	Motion sickness	Fungal infections
Lack of concentration	Muscular aches and pains	Psoriasis
Moodiness	Nervousness, tension, stress	Stretch marks
Nervous tension	Respiratory conditions (including	Varicose veins
Panic attacks	colds, flu, sore throat, asthma,	Wrinkles
Poor memory	and bronchitis)	
Sadness	Skin inflammation	
Worry	Wounds and scars	

The most troublesome task will be flushing out the system and ridding it of accumulated scale. Some steam generators have automatic flushing systems that drain the water after each use so that fresh water is heated each time the steam bath is used. Others, however, require manual flushing to remove sediment at the bottom of the unit. This should be done once a month, or more frequently if your water is hard and/or your steam bath gets a lot of use. Typically, a steam generator can be flushed by following these procedures:

1. *Allow the generator to cool down if it's been running.*

2. *Press the ON button to start water flowing into the generator.*

3. *Open the manual drain valve.*

4. *Allow the water to run through the unit for 10 minutes.*

5. *Press the OFF button.*

6. *When the water stops flowing out of the drain, close the manual drain valve.*

Manufacturers may have different techniques for flushing the system. Be sure to consult the owner's manual for your steam generator to obtain the specific procedures for your unit.

Over time, all steam generators will develop scale. How long that takes depends on how soft or hard the water is and how often the steam generator operates. As water is heated, calcium and other minerals can fall out of solution and coat the inside of the steam generator and plumbing. There are different procedures for descaling a steam generator, depending on whether it has an automatic or manual flushing system. Your owner's manual will detail the procedures for your unit. Manufacturers often advise that homeowners call in a service professional and not undertake this task themselves.

Removing the scale from a steam generator isn't all that different from eliminating scale from a coffeemaker. It should be done at least once a year — more often if the water source is hard and/or the steam bath is used a lot. In fact, a steam generator that uses very hard water may need to be descaled up to 20 times more frequently than a generator that uses extremely soft water.

Generally, the descaling process calls for filling the water reservoir with water, allowing

▲ Limestone walls and tile mosaics add old-world charm and elegance to this spacious steam bath.

it to heat up, and then adding a descaling product to the water. This removes calcium and any other deposits that have become encrusted on the walls of the water reservoir and the heating element. After giving the descaler time to work (no more than one hour), the solution is thoroughly flushed from the system by draining the reservoir and allowing fresh water to run through it.

With some routine cleaning and maintenance, your steam bath will reward you with years of trouble-free enjoyment. That means less time worrying and more time relaxing in your steamy retreat.

TROUBLESHOOTING COMMON STEAM BATH PROBLEMS

The heart of the steam bath is the steam generator, and that is where you are most likely to encounter some problems. Though most major brands of steam generators are incredibly durable, their dependability is subject to factors beyond their control, such as proper installation, water quality, and routine maintenance.

If the steam generator doesn't perform well immediately after it has been installed, check to make sure the control panel and steam generator are installed and wired according to the manufacturer's directions and wiring diagram. Also make sure that the drainage pipe slopes properly and doesn't have any sags.

Your first clues that something might be wrong are a delay in the heat-up time and a change in steam pressure. Over time, some of the most common problems have to do with calcium buildup in the reservoir, a faulty temperature sensor, a problematic solenoid valve, or a blocked steam pipe. Here are a few tests you can perform to determine whether any of these problems exist.

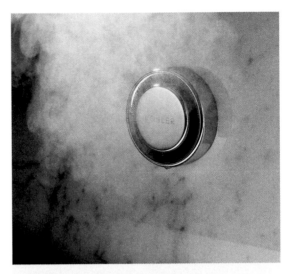

▲ Steam enters the bath or shower via a steam head. Most steam heads include a small reservoir on the top for fragrant oils, which are carried by the steam to create an aromatherapy experience.

Calcium Deposits in the Reservoir

Unscrew the capping nut at the top of the steam generator and peer inside, using a flashlight to illuminate the inside of the reservoir. If there is substantial buildup of calcium carbonate, the unit may not have been routinely descaled per the manufacturer's instructions. (Read about descaling procedures on the facing page.)

Another possibility is that the flushing and drainage system isn't working properly. Check to see whether the automatic emptying function (if there is one) is working by placing a bucket underneath the drainage valve. Turn on the steam generator and let it run for about 15 minutes, and then switch it off from the control panel. If the unit hasn't drained after 80 minutes or so, the steam generator may not have been wired correctly, or the power to the generator is being interrupted somehow. There could also be a fault in the drainage valve or circuit, which should be repaired by a professional service technician.

Common Steam Bath Problems

If you encounter a problem with your steam bath, the problem probably resides with the steam generator. You may be able to address some issues yourself, but most will require professional repair service.

PROBLEM	CAUSE	SOLUTION
Control panel won't turn on.	There is no power.	Make sure the circuit breaker is on. If it is, use a voltmeter to make sure the unit is receiving the correct voltage. Check the fuses and replace them if they are blown.
	There is a faulty connection.	Make sure the controls are installed per the manufacturer's guidelines.
	The control cables are faulty.	Replace control cables.
	The control panel is faulty.	Replace control panel.
Control is off, but water won't shut off and runs out of the steam head.	Water valve is stuck open.	Turn off the circuit breaker and call in a service professional.
Steam bath is too hot or too cold.	Temperature setting needs to be adjusted.	See instructions in the owner's manual.
Steam bath maintains the desired temperature but no steam is produced.	The air coming into the steam bath is too warm.	Reduce the intake air temperature to 95°F (35°C) or less, possibly by opening a window or turning on air-conditioning.
	The ambient temperature is too warm.	Reduce the ambient air temperature to 95°F (35°C) or less, possibly by opening a window or turning on air-conditioning.
	The thermometer is faulty or placed in the wrong spot.	The thermometer should be placed about 67 inches (170 cm) above the floor and as far away from the steam head as possible.

PROBLEM	CAUSE	SOLUTION
The steam bath takes a long time to heat up.	There is too much ventilation of the steam bath.	Reduce the ventilation by keeping the door to the bath closed except when absolutely necessary.
	The ambient temperature is lower than 60°F (15°C).	Increase the ambient air temperature by heating the exterior room.
	The heating element is broken.	Replace it.
	The thermostat sensor is too close to the steam head.	Move the sensor or change the direction of the steam head away from the sensor.
Hot water runs from the steam head, but no steam is produced.	The solenoid valve for incoming water is stuck due to accumulated deposits.	Remove the valve and clean it.
	The solenoid valve is broken.	Replace the valve.
	There's a malfunction in the circuit board.	Replace the circuit board.
Hot water spurts from the steam head.	The steam pipe is not insulated and/or is too long, causing steam to condense.	Insulate the steam pipe.
	There are foaming contaminants in the water.	Flush the tank three times. If the problem persists, call a service technician.
Hot water continuously trickles from the drainage pipe.	The solenoid valve for automatically flushing the reservoir is stuck.	Remove and clean the valve.

▲ A simple control panel turns the steam generator on and off and also sets the desired temperature.

Faulty Temperature Sensor

To test whether the temperature sensor is malfunctioning, simply soak a small towel in cold water and hang it over the thermostat sensor. This will ensure that the sensor is cool enough for the steam generator to turn on, Activate the steam generator. If it starts to produce steam in the normal time frame, the sensor is not broken, but it may be located too close to the steam head. When this happens, the sensor heats up faster than the rest of the steam bath, and it shuts off the steam generator prematurely. Do what you can to relocate the temperature sensor as far away from the steam head as possible. However, if it is wired through a tiled wall or other permanent installation, you might have to raise the temperature setting at the control panel to achieve the true temperature you want. If the sensor is faulty, you'll need to order a new one from the manufacturer and connect it yourself or have an electrician do it for you.

Faulty Solenoid Valve

Use the control panel to switch off the steam generator. If water continues to trickle out of the steam head more than 10 minutes after the control panel has been switched off, the cause is probably dirt in the solenoid valve. Remove and clean the valve. If the water stops running through the steam head within 10 minutes after the control panel has been switched off, the cause is probably a faulty connection or circuit board. It also might mean that excessive calcium carbonate has accumulated in the reservoir.

Blocked Steam Pipe

Sometimes when the safety valve or the temperature cut-off switch is activated, it means the steam pipe is blocked. To test whether this is the case, disconnect the steam pipe from the steam generator and turn it on for at least one hour. If the safety valve or temperature cut-off switch is not triggered during this time, there is probably a blockage in the pipe that is causing the problem. This means that something in the pipe is preventing the steam from traveling from the generator to the steam head, and the blockage needs to be removed.

Before you call in the service professionals, check the table on page 135 to see whether you can troubleshoot and repair any problems yourself. Keep in mind, however, that all plumbing and electrical work should be done by a licensed professional, especially if you don't want to void your product's warranty.

GLOSSARY

Accessible. Easily exposed for inspection and the replacement of materials and/or parts with the use of tools.

Acid. A liquid or dry compound used to reduce the pH of spa water, such as sodium bisulfate or muriatic acid.

Acrylic. A thermoplastic sheet vacuum-formed into a mold to make a spa.

Air blower. A mechanical device that forces air through holes in the floor or hydrotherapy jets in a spa.

Algae. Microscopic plantlike organisms that contain chlorophyll. Algae are nourished by carbon dioxide (CO_2) and use sunlight to carry out photosynthesis. They are introduced to pools and spas by rain or wind and grow in colonies. Algae don't cause disease, but they can harbor bacteria. The most common spa and pool types are black, blue-green, green, and mustard (yellow or brown). Maintaining proper sanitizer levels, shocking, and superchlorination will help prevent their occurrence.

Algicide. A natural or synthetic substance used for killing, destroying, or controlling algae.

Alkali (base). A class of compounds that will react with an acid to produce a salt. Alkali is the opposite of acid.

Alkalinity. More commonly called total alkalinity; a measure of the pH-buffering capacity of water (the water's resistance to change in pH). An indicator of the hydroxides, carbonates, and bicarbonates in the water. One of the basic water tests necessary to determine water balance.

Ambient room temperature. The air temperature surrounding a steam bath when not in use.

Antifoam. A chemical added to water to make suds or foam go away. Antifoam products do not remove the source of the foaming. Most often, the water must be drained and refilled to remove the soaps, oils, and other causes of foaming.

Available chlorine. The amount of chlorine, both free and combined, in water that is available to sanitize or disinfect the water.

Avanto. A Finnish word meaning a hole in the ice of a frozen lake or sea.

Avantouinti. A Finnish word loosely meaning "ice hole swimming," describing the process in which swimmers cut a large opening through the ice (*avanto*) and either take a quick plunge or swim for a few minutes.

Bacteria. Single-celled microorganisms of various forms, some of which are undesirable or potentially disease causing. Bacteria are controlled by chlorine, bromine, and other sanitizing and disinfecting agents.

Baking soda. Chemically called sodium bicarbonate. It is a white powder used to raise the total alkalinity of spa water without having much affect on pH.

Balanced water. Water having the correct ratio of mineral content and pH level that prevents the water from being corrosive or scale forming.

Base (basic). A class of compounds that will react with an acid to produce a salt. Base is the opposite of acid.

Bather. A user of a spa, sauna, or steam bath.

Bather load. The number of bathers combined with bathing duration and frequency.

Blower. An electrical device that produces a continuous rush of air to create the optimal bubbling effect in a spa, hot tub, or whirlpool. It is usually plumbed in with the hydrotherapy jets or to a separate bubbler ring.

Bromamines. By-products formed when bromine reacts with bather waste (perspiration or urine, body oils, soaps, etc.). Bromamines are active disinfectants and do not smell, although high levels can cause skin irritation. Bromamines are removed by superchlorination or shock treatment.

Bromide. A common term for a bromide salt used to supply bromide ions to the water so they may be oxidized or changed into hypobromous acid, the killing form of bromine. Used as a disinfectant.

Brominator. A mechanical or electrical device for dispensing bromine at a controlled rate. Most often a canister or floater filled with tablets of bromine.

Bromine. A disinfectant that destroys bacteria and algae in spas.

Btu. Abbreviation for British thermal unit. The amount of heat necessary to raise one pound of water one degree Fahrenheit.

Buffer. A substance or compound that stabilizes pH value. It is also the water's resistance to change in pH.

Calcium carbonate (scale). The crystalline compounds formed in water when the calcium, pH, and total alkalinity levels are too high. Once formed, the crystals adhere to the plumbing, equipment, and other surfaces.

Calcium chloride. A soluble white salt used to raise the calcium or total hardness level in spa water.

Calcium hardness. The calcium content of the water. Calcium hardness is sometimes confused with the terms *water hardness* and *total hardness*. Too little calcium hardness and the water is corrosive. Too much calcium hardness and the water is scale forming. Testing for calcium hardness is one of the basic ways to determine water balance.

Calcium hypochlorite. A compound of chlorine and calcium used as a disinfectant, sanitizer, bactericide, algicide, and oxidizer in spa water. It is available as a white granular material usually used for superchlorination or as tablets used in a feeder for regular chlorination.

Cartridge filter. A water filter that uses a disposable porous element made of paper or polyester.

Chelate (sequester). The process of preventing metals in water from combining with other components in the water to form colored precipitates that stain spa walls and bottoms or produce colored water.

Chemical feeder. Any of several types of devices that dispense chemicals into spa water at a predetermined rate. Some dispense sanitizers while others dispense pH-adjusting chemicals.

Chloramines. Undesirable, foul-smelling, body-irritating compounds formed when insufficient levels of free available chlorine react with ammonia and other nitrogen-containing compounds (swimmer and bather waste, fertilizer, perspiration, urine, etc.). Chloramines are still disinfectants, but they are a much weaker, ineffective form of chlorine. Chloramines are removed by superchlorination or shock treatment.

Chlorinator. A mechanical or electrical device for dispensing chlorine at a controlled rate. Most often a canister or floater filled with tablets of chlorine.

Chlorine. A chemical element used to disinfect water.

Chlorine generator. An electrical device that generates chlorine from a salt solution in a tank or from salt added to spa water.

Chlorine residual. The amount of chlorine left in spa water after the chlorine demand has been satisfied.

Circulation equipment. The mechanical components of a spa circulation system, including pumps, filters, valves, heaters, inlet/outlet fittings, and chemical feeders.

Clarifier (coagulant, flocculant). A chemical compound that gathers suspended particles together so they can be removed by vacuuming or filtration.

Coagulant. An organic polyelectrolyte used to gather suspended particles in water so they can be removed by vacuuming or filtration.

Combined chlorine. The total amount of chloramines and available chlorine in water. Combined chlorine still disinfects, but it isn't very effective.

Corrosion. The etching, pitting or eating away of equipment or fixtures. Caused by improper water balance, misuse of acid or acidic products, or soft water.

Covers. Something that covers, protects, and/or shelters a spa.

Cubic feet. The three-dimensional measurement of a linear foot.

Deck. The area adjacent to or surrounding a spa used for sitting, standing, or walking.

Diatomaceous earth filter. A filter that utilizes a thin coating of diatomaceous earth (DE) over a porous fabric as its filter medium. Diatomaceous earth is composed of microscopic fossil skeletons of the diatom, a tiny freshwater marine plankton.

Filter. A device that removes undissolved or suspended particles from water by recirculating the water through a porous substance. The most popular type of filter used in self-contained spas is a cartridge filter.

Filter cartridge. A replaceable porous element made of paper or polyester used as the filter medium in cartridge filters.

Filter cycle. The operating time between a spa's cleaning cycles.

Filter medium. A finely graded material such as sand, diatomaceous earth, polyester fabric, or anthracite that removes filterable particles from the water.

Flocculating agent (flocculant). A chemical substance or compound that promotes the combination, agglomeration, or coagulation of suspended particles in water so they can be filtered out.

Flow rate. The quantity of water flowing past a designated point within a specified time.

Foam. A froth of bubbles on the surface of water. Usually comes from soap, oil, deodorant, hair spray, and suntan oil, that is shed into the water as swimmers enter.

Free available chlorine. That portion of the total chlorine remaining in chlorinated water that is not combined with ammonia or nitrogen compounds and will react chemically with undesirable or pathogenic organisms.

Grab rail. Tubular rails that bathers can grasp for assistance in entering or leaving a spa, usually made of stainless steel or chrome-plated brass.

Ground fault circuit interrupter (GFCI). A device that interrupts the electrical circuit whenever it detects the presence of excess electrical current going to ground.

Halogens. The chemical elements either individually or collectively that constitute group VIIB of the periodic table of elements: fluorine, chlorine, bromine, iodine, and astatine. Of these, only chlorine and bromine are used as disinfectants and sanitizers in spas.

Handrail. A tubular steel or plastic device that can be gripped by swimmers or bathers for the purpose of steadying themselves.

Hardness. The amount of calcium and magnesium dissolved in water; measured by a test kit and expressed as parts per million of equivalent calcium carbonate.

Heater. Typically an electric device used to heat spa water. Electric heaters use a heating element immersed in water.

Horsepower. A measure of work done per unit of time. One horsepower is equal to 33,000 foot-pounds of work per minute or approximately 746 watts. Motors for pumps are rated in horsepower.

Hot tub. Originally, a construction of wood with the sides and bottom formed separately and joined together by hoops, bands, or rods. However, the word has become synonymous with *spa*, which is acrylic, fiberglass, concrete, or metal.

Hydrochloric acid (muriatic acid). A strong acid used to lower pH and total alkalinity. It can also be used for various cleaning needs. Used in acid washing a pool. Use extreme care in handling.

Hydrogen peroxide. An unstable, colorless, heavy liquid used as an oxidizing agent in spas. May also be used to dechlorinate spa water.

Hydrotherapy jet. A fitting in a spa on the water return line that mixes air and water, creating a high-velocity, turbulent stream of water.

Hypobromous acid. The most powerful disinfecting form of bromine in water.

Hypochlorous acid. The most powerful disinfecting form of chlorine in water.

Impeller. The rotating vanes of a centrifugal pump; its action creates the flow of water.

Infrared. Electromagnetic radiation with wavelengths greater than those of visible light.

Ionizer. A water-sanitation device that uses electricity to generate metal ions, which are dispersed in the water. It works by passing a low-voltage DC current through a set of metallic (usually copper and silver) electrodes placed in-line with the circulation equipment. The copper is an algaecide, while the silver is a bactericide. Does not remove swimmer waste.

Jacuzzi. A brand name of a spa or whirlpool.

Jet. A spa fitting where water is returned to the vessel.

Kilowatt. Equal to 1,000 watts. It is the universal measure of electric steam generators.

Kippo (kauha). A Finnish word that refers to a ladle used to throw water on the hot sauna rocks.

Kiua. A Finnish word that refers a sauna stove or heater.

Kiulu. A Finnish word that refers to a small pail or bucket that contains the *löyly* water. It is usually made of wooden boards secured with wooden hoops.

Lakeinen. A Finnish word that refers to the opening in the ceiling of a smoke sauna through which the smoke escapes during heating.

Lautee. A Finnish word that refers the elevated platform or benches in the sauna. Heat rises, so this is the place to relax when seeking the hottest temperatures.

Lithium hypochlorite. A dry, granular chlorinating compound with an available chlorine content of 35 percent. It dissolves quickly and can be used to superchlorinate spas and hot tubs.

Löyly. A Finnish word for the steam or vapor created by throwing water on the heated stones.

Muriatic acid. Used to lower pH and/or total alkalinity in spa water.

Nonchlorine shock. A term given to a class of chemical compounds that are used to oxidize or shock water without the use of chlorine or bromine.

Organic waste (bather waste). All of the soap, deodorant, sunscreen, makeup, cologne, body oils, sweat, urine, etc., brought into the water by bathers. They form chloramines, which are foul-smelling body irritants. They require large amounts of chlorine or nonchlorine shock to destroy.

Oxidation. The process of purging the water of ammonia, nitrogen compounds, and bather waste through superchlorination or shock treatment with a nonchlorine oxidizer.

Ozonator. Electrical devices that produce ozone from air or oxygen. The ozone is injected into the water, where it oxidizes contaminants.

PH. A term used to indicate the level of acidity or alkalinity of spa water. The pH scale ranges from 0 to 14, with 7 being neutral. Too low pH causes corrosion, and too high pH causes scale formation.

Potassium monopersulfate. A nonchlorine oxidizer. It does not kill bacteria or algae, but it will oxidize or destroy ammonia, nitrogen, and bather waste. It has a low pH, and it does not increase chlorine or bromine levels the way that superchlorination does, so bathers may enter the water 15 minutes after its addition. It will also reactivate bromine to its killing form, hypobromous acid.

ppm. An abbreviation for parts per million. It is a weight-to-weight expression. It means 1 part in 1 million parts.

Pukuhuone. The finish word for dressing room.

Pump. A piece of equipment powered by an electric motor that causes water to flow through the circulation system of a spa for filtration, heating, and circulation.

Pump capacity. The volume of liquid a pump is capable of moving during a specified period of time. This is usually stated in gallons per minute (gpm).

Räppänä. A Finnish word that refers to the duct or vent on the sauna wall close to the ceiling.

Residual bromine. The amount of bromine left in the spa water after the bromine demand has been satisfied.

Residual chlorine. The amount of chlorine left in the spa water after the chlorine demand has been satisfied.

Sanitize. To render sanitary; to kill all living things, including bacteria and algae.

Sauna. A Finnish-style sweat bath or the room where the bath occurs. The correct pronunciation is sow-na (as in "cow"), not saw-na.

Savusauna. A Finnish word for a smoke sauna, which is the original form of sauna, with no chimney.

Scale. The precipitate that forms on surfaces in contact with water when the calcium hardness, pH, or total alkalinity levels are too high.

Scum. Foreign matter that rises to the surface of the water and forms a layer of film. It can also be a residue deposited along the waterline of a spa. Sources of scum are soap, oil, deodorant, hair spray, suntan lotion, and other contaminants.

Sequestering agent (chelating agent). A chemical that combines with dissolved metals in the water to prevent the metals from coming out of solution and causing stains.

Shock treatment. The practice of adding significant amounts of an oxidizing chemical to water to destroy ammonia and nitrogenous and organic contaminants.

Soda ash (sodium carbonate). A chemical used to raise the pH and total alkalinity in water.

Sodium bicarbonate (baking soda). A chemical used to raise total alkalinity in spa water with only a slight effect on the pH.

Sodium bisulfate. A granule used to lower pH and/or total alkalinity in water.

Steam generator reservoir. The assembly inside the steam generator that houses the heating element and necessary water to make steam.

Test kit. A device used to monitor specific chemical residuals or demands in spa water.

Test strips. Small plastic strips with pads attached that have been impregnated with reagents that can be used to test spa water for chemical residuals or demands. The strips are usually dipped in the water, and the resulting colors of the pads are compared to a standard set of colors to determine concentration.

Thermal cover. An insulating cover used to prevent evaporation and heat loss from spas.

Total alkalinity. The ability or capacity of water to resist change in pH; also known as the buffering capacity of the water. Measured with a test kit and expressed as ppm.

Total chlorine. The sum of both the free available and the combined chlorines.

Total dissolved solids (TDS). A measure of the total amount of dissolved matter in water.

Turnover rate. The period of time (usually in hours) required to circulate a volume of water equal to the spa capacity.

Underwater light. A fixture designed to illuminate a spa from beneath the water surface.

Vihta (vasta). A Finnish word for a thick bunch of birch twigs used to swat oneself to promote blood circulation and cleanse the skin.

Waterline. The height to which the water is filled in a spa. This is usually in the middle of the skimmer opening or the center of the waterline tile.

Selecting a Retailer, Installer, or Contractor

Installing your own hot tub, sauna, or steam bath can be a daunting challenge depending on how handy you are with light construction, electrical, and plumbing work. In most cases, homeowners choose to call in the professionals. You'll pay handsomely for the skilled labor, but the peace of mind you'll have is typically well worth the expense. Plus, if a mistake is made during installation, you'll have someone other than yourself to hold accountable.

In most cases, retailers who sell prefabricated hot tubs, saunas, and steam baths also provide installation services. For custom jobs, however, you'll probably have to line up a contractor on your own. Before you crack open the phone book in search of the ideal company, make sure you know what you're looking for. Here are some questions to get you started:

● **Does the dealer have a showroom?** If someone is selling hot tubs out of his residential garage, chances are he might not be around to handle problems down the road. Traditionally, businesses with professional showrooms have superior product knowledge and customer service than those who work out of a home office or the back of a truck.

● **How long has the company been in business?** A lot of businesses fail within their first five years of operation, so pick a dealer or contractor who has a long and profitable history in the community. You

might make an exception for someone who built up years of experience working for a competitor before launching his own business. But avoid companies that have filed for bankruptcy protection under either their current name or a previous name.

● **Are the installer, general contractor, and subcontractors adequately insured?** If someone gets hurt or your property gets damaged during installation and construction, you want to make sure the damages are covered by someone else's insurance policy. Consider asking for a certificate of insurance if you have any concerns.

● **Are there any unresolved complaints against the company?** The Better Business Bureau logs customer complaints and may be able to provide information on the companies you're considering.

● **Does the company belong to any professional associations or trade groups?** The more professional and qualified businesses tend to belong to guilds and organizations that help them stay abreast of changing technologies, regulations, market trends, and other topics of concern. Though membership in such groups is no guarantee of quality work, it usually helps.

● **How many projects like yours has this company worked on?** When it comes to hot tub, sauna, and steam bath installation, nothing beats experience. Who would you rather hire to install your steam generator: a novice plumber who has installed 10 steam units in the past year or a 20-year veteran of kitchen and bath plumbing who has never installed a steam unit? Every installation is somewhat unique, but someone who has worked on many similar projects is probably prepared to solve any problems that arise on your project. Ask to see the installer's portfolio so you can see whether your project is in line with the type and quality of work presented.

● *Who are some recent clients?* Interviewing past customers is a great way to gauge a company's performance. However, don't simply ask for the names of three customers you can talk with, because you'll be given the names of three customers who are prepared to rave about the company. Instead, ask to speak with the company's three most recent customers. Alternatively, ask to speak with one customer from each of the past three months. Then contact each customer and ask about his or her experience before, during, and after the sale. What problems arose? How satisfied were they with the results? Would they recommend this company? Better yet, would they hire them again?

Finally, use your best instincts. If two of your friends have purchased a sauna from the same dealer and they both have had trouble-free experiences, that might be all the proof you need. Indeed, anytime a friend or colleague gives you an enthusiastic referral, that speaks louder than anything else.

APPENDIX B

Resource List

Spa Suppliers

ARISTECH ACRYLICS LLC
7350 Empire Drive
Florence, KY 41042
www.thedreamhome.com
(800) 354-9858

CAL SPAS
1462 E. Ninth Street
Pomona, CA 91766
www.calspas.com
(800) 225-7727

COLEMAN SPAS BY MAAX
25605 S. Arizona Avenue
Chandler, AZ 85248
www.colemanspas.com
(800) 367-4286

DIMENSION ONE SPAS
2611 Business Park Drive
Vista, CA 92081
www.d1spas.com
(800) 345-7727

EMERALD SPA CORP.
4150 E. Paris S.E.
Kentwood, MI 49512
www.emeraldspa.com
(800) 766-7727

GREAT LAKES HOME & RESORT
935 East 40th Street
Holland, MI 49423
www.greatlakeshomeandresort.com
(800) 458-1476

JACUZZI PREMIUM
14525 Monte Vista Avenue
Chino, CA 91710
www.jacuzzipremium.com
(866) 924-7727

L.A. SPAS/ADVANCED SPA DESIGN
1311 N. Blue Gum Street
Anaheim, CA 92806
www.laspas.com
(714) 630-1150

LEISURE BAY INDUSTRIES
3033 Mercy Drive
Orlando, FL 32808
www.leisurebay.com
(888) 524-9475

MARQUIS CORP.
596 Hoffman Road
Independence, OR 97351
www.marquisspas.com
(800) 275-0888

MASTER SPAS
6927 Lincoln Parkway
Fort Wayne, IN 46804
www.masterspas.com
(888) 552-7727

PDC SPAS
75 Palmer Industrial Road
Williamsport, PA 17701
www.pdcspas.com
(800) 451-1420

POOLANDSPA.COM
12 Old Dock Road
Yaphank, NY 11980
www.poolandspa.com
(800) 876-7647

SOFTUB INC.
27615 Avenue Hopkins
Valencia, CA 91355
www.softub.com
(661) 702-1401

SPRINT AQUATICS
P. O. Box 3840
San Luis Obispo, CA 93403
www.sprintaquatics.com
(800) 235-2156

SUNDANCE SPAS INC.
14525 Monte Vista Avenue
Chino, CA 91710
www.sundancespas.com
(800) 883-7727

THERMOSPAS INC.
155 East Street
Wallingford, CT 06492
www.thermospas.com
(800) 876-0158

VITA INTERNATIONAL
2320 N.W. 147th Street
Miami, FL 33054
www.vitaspa.com
(800) 848-2772

**WATKINS MFG./
HOT SPRING SPAS**
1280 Park Center Drive
Vista, CA 92081
www.hotspring.com
(800) 999-4688

Sauna Suppliers

AIRMIST SAUNA & STEAM
52 Hamel Road
Hamel, MN 55340
www.airmist.com
(800) 728-6226

AMEREC PRODUCTS
17683 128th Place N.E.
Woodinville, WA 98072
www.amerec.com
(800) 331-0349

AM-FINN SAUNA CO.
P. O. Box 29406
Greensboro, NC 27429
www.am-finnsauna.com
(800) 237-2862

**BALTIC LEISURE,
DIV. OF PENN SAUNA**
601 Lincoln Street
Oxford, PA 19363-0530
www.balticleisure.com
(800) 441-7147

CALLAWAY WOODWORKS
11320-A FM 529
Houston, TX 77041
www.redwoodsaunas.com
(877) 518-9698

CAL SPAS
1462 E. Ninth Street
Pomona, CA 91766
www.calspas.com
(800) 225-7727

**CEDARBROOK SAUNA
& STEAM USA**
P. O. Box 535
Cashmere, WA 98815
www.saunasauna.com
(800) 634-6334

**FINLANDIA/HARVIA
SAUNA PRODUCTS**
14010-B S.W. 72nd Avenue
Portland, OR 97224
www.finlandiasauna.com
(800) 354-3342

FINNISH AMERICAN SAUNA CO.
871 Charter Street
Redwood City, CA 94063-3004
(650) 327-5001

FINNLEO SAUNA & STEAM
575 E. Cokato Street
Cokato, MN 55321
www.finnleo.com
(800) 346-6536

HELO SAUNA & STEAM
575 E. Cokato Street
Cokato, MN 55321
www.helosaunas.com
(800) 882-4352

SUSSMAN LIFESTYLE GROUP
43-20 34th Street
Long Island City, NY 11101
www.mrsteam.com
(800) 767-8326

THERASAUNA
1021 State Street
Bettendorf, IA 52722
www.therasauna.com
(888) 729-7727

THERMASOL
2255 Union Place
Simi Valley, CA 93065
www.thermasol.com
(800) 776-0711

Steam Bath Suppliers

AIRMIST SAUNA & STEAM
52 Hamel Road
P.O. Box 297
Hamel, MN 55340
www.airmist.com
(800) 728-6226

AMEREC PRODUCTS
17683 128th Place N.E.
Woodinville, WA 98072
www.amerec.com
(800) 331-0349

ELECTRO-STEAM GENERATOR CORP.
1000 Bernard Street
Alexandria, VA 22314-1223
www.electrosteam.com
(800) 634-8177

FINNLEO SAUNA & STEAM
575 E. Cokato Street
Cokato, MN 55321
www.finnleo.com
(800) 346-6536

HELO SAUNA & STEAM
575 E. Cokato Street
Cokato, MN 55321
www.helosaunas.com
(800) 882-4352

JACUZZI WHIRLPOOL BATH
2121 N. California Boulevard
Walnut Creek, CA 94596
www.jacuzzi.com
(925) 938-7070

STEAMSAUNABATH
855 Laurel Avenue
Belmont, CA 94002
steamsaunabath.com
(800) 707-2862

SUSSMAN LIFESTYLE GROUP
43-20 34th Street
Long Island City, NY 11101
www.mrsteam.com
(800) 767-8326

THERMASOL
2255 Union Place
Simi Valley, CA 93065
www.thermasol.com
(800) 776-0711

Associations

ARTHRITIS FOUNDATION
www.arthritis.org
(800) 283-7800

Among this group's consumer resources are *Water Exercise: Pools, Spas and Arthritis,* a 20-page brochure on why water exercise is a safe, ideal environment for relieving arthritis pain and stiffness. Sponsored by the makers of Hot Spring Spas, the brochure includes purchasing tips, medical precautions, and exercises for pools or hot tubs. Also available is a companion piece, *Make Waves: A Warm-Water Workout,* a laminated card that includes safety tips and illustrated water exercises. The first copy of each is free.

ASSOCIATION OF POOL AND SPA PROFESSIONALS (APSP)
www.theapsp.org
www.hottubliving.com
(703) 838-008

APSP is the world's largest trade association representing the swimming pool, spa, hot tub, and recreational water industries. It offers information on hot tub ownership and safety, and it directs consumers to member companies in their area. It also operates the HotTubLiving.com Web site, which offers hot tub buying advice.

THE FINNISH SAUNA SOCIETY
www.sauna.fi
358-9-6860-560

Located in Helsinki, Finland, the Finnish Sauna Society is a private cultural association founded in 1937 to foster the heritage of the national bath. Its primary function is to preserve the traditional native sauna culture, spread information about it, correct wrong impressions about the sauna, emphasize the meaning of sauna bathing for a healthy life, and develop the sauna of the present day. To achieve its goals the society, among other things, publishes information in various forms, organizes seminars and symposiums, supports and initiates scientific research, and maintains a traditional sauna for its members. In 1977, the group initiated the International Sauna Society (ISS), whose purpose is to promote sauna use worldwide.

INTERNATIONAL SPA ASSOCIATION (ISPA)
www.experienceispa.com
(888) 226-4326

ISPA defines the spa experience as "your time to relax, reflect, revitalize, and rejoice." Though the organization's main emphasis is on destination spas, its Web site does offer trend and lifestyle information of interest to anyone trying to create a spa experience in his or her own home — including recipes for spa cuisine.

NATIONAL KITCHEN & BATH ASSOCIATION (NKBA)
www.nkba.com
(877) NKBA-PRO

Group that offers tips, tools, and ideas for homeowners looking to build or remodel kitchens and bathrooms. NKBA also lists member professionals who can assist with these projects.

Magazines

AQUA MAGAZINE
www.aquamagazine.com

This monthly trade magazine offers an online directory that includes manufacturers of hot tubs, saunas, and steam baths, often with links to the manufacturers' Web sites.

POOL & SPA LIVING
www.poolspaliving.com

Available at large newsstands, *Pool & Spa Living* is the leading consumer magazine devoted to swimming pools, hot tub, spas, and the accompanying lifestyle. The magazine covers what's new in pools, hot tubs, portable spas, swim spas, and saunas, as well as care and safety. The Web site provides free access to select articles. Its sister publication, *America's Top Hot Tubs & Spas,* offers consumers a way to compare top brands before they buy.

POOL & SPA NEWS
www.poolspanews.com

This bi-monthly trade magazine offers an online directory that includes manufacturers of hot tubs, saunas, and steam baths, often with links to the manufacturers' Web sites.

PHOTO CREDITS

INDEX

showers and, 129, *129*
size, 116, *117*
skylights, 118
solenoid valve in, 136
sound systems, 109
steam generator effectiveness and
    design of, 122
steam generators in, 109, 113–14, 120,
    122, 129–33
steam heads, *118, 133*
steam pipe blocked in, 136
style, *124*
suppliers, 145
temperature range, 127
temperature sensor in, 136
tile, *107*, 117, *132*
transom, hinged for, *128*
troubleshooting, 133–36
ventilation, *128*
water lines, 113
windows, 118, *120*
Steam generators, *113*, 113–14, 129–33
    aromatherapy reservoir in, 120
    control panel for, *136*
    descaling, 132–33
    flushing, 132
    installation location of, 120–21, *121*
    kilowatt rating of, 122
    noise, 114, 120
    size, 113–14, 120
    sizing, **122,** 122–23, **123**
    soft steam from, 120
    steam line, 121
    steam room design and effectiveness of, 122
    temperature produced by, 113
    voltage, 113, 122
Swim spas, 12, 16–17, *17*, 31

T

TDS. *See* Total dissolved solids
Televisions
    hot tub, *33, 36*
    sauna, *79*
Temperatures
    hot tubs, 18, 36, 40, 45
    sanitation and, 45

saunas, 75–76, 77
steam baths, 127, 136
steam generator-produces, 113
Total dissolved solids (TDS), 40, 45
Troubleshooting
    cartridge filter, 59
    hot tub, 57–65
    hot tub heater, 65
    hot tub water, *56*
    pump problem, 62–63
    sauna, 100–101
    steam bath, 133–36
Turkish baths, *2*, 107, *107*

V

Vapor barriers, 28
Vihta (birch branches), *95, 96, 97*

W

Water balance, 40–47, **46,** 54
Water chemicals, 57–58
Water problem troubleshooting, *56*
Water testing, 42–43
Water volume, 39, 40

OTHER STOREY TITLES YOU WILL ENJOY

What Color Is Your Swimming Pool? *by Alan E. Sanderfoot*
Forever banish cloudy waters, sprouting algae, funky odors, and corroding equipment using this completely updated edition of the best-selling, easy-to-follow handbook that covers everything from basic water treatment to solar heating and features an expanded chapter on spas and hot tubs. 144 pages. Paperback. ISBN 1-58017-309-8.

Poolscaping *by Catriona Tudor Erler*
This comprehensive resource overflows with inspiring ideas and practical advice on how to landscape around your swimming pool, spa, or hot tub to create your own private resort. 208 pages. Paperback. ISBN 1-58017-385-3.

The Aromatherapy Companion *by Victoria H. Edwards*
Discover the healing benefits of aromatherapy with hundreds of soothing recipes for beauty, health, and emotional well-being through every stage of life. 288 pages. Paperback. ISBN 1-58017-150-8.

The Essential Oils Book *by Colleen K. Dodt*
Fragrant essences lift the spirits, stimulate the senses, and enhance relaxation after a trying day. This practical guide shows how essential oils — used at home and on the go — can greatly improve the quality of busy lives. 160 pages. Paperback. ISBN 0-88266-913-3.

The Modular Home *by Andrew Gianino*
Advice for the prospective modular home (or modular addition) buyer or builder on everything from choosing a floor plan and buying the home to finding the right contractor and selecting customization options. 328 pages. Paperback. ISBN 1-58017-526-0.

Dream Cottages *by Catherine Tredway*
25 unique design plans for a variety of cottages, with customized floor plans and architectural features. Elegantly illustrated by the author, an architect. 176 pages. Paperback. ISBN 1-58017-372-1.

These books and other Storey books are available wherever books are sold and directly from Storey Publishing, 210 MASS MoCA Way, North Adams, MA 01247, or by calling 1-800-441-5700. www.storey.com